Build Complete
Confidence with Horses

Build Complete Confidence with Horses

Beat Fear and Excuses & Attain Your Riding Goals

Kelly Marks

TRAFALGAR SQUARE
North Pomfret, Vermont

For my dad, Douglas Marks
(8 May 1922–7 June 2007)

First published in the United States of America in 2007 by
Trafalgar Square Books
North Pomfret, Vermont 05053

Printed and bound by Italy

ISBN: 978-1-57076-373-1

Library of Congress Control Number: 2007928701

See page 224 for a complete list of picture credits.

10 9 8 7 6 5 4 3 2 1

Contents

Monty Roberts

In the summer of 1995 I was in England to work with some thoroughbred racehorses that were proving to be difficult at the starting stalls. I had previously made arrangements with Kelly Marks, the daughter of Douglas Marks, a long-standing Lambourn trainer, to assist me in organizing demonstrations of my work.

Kelly had recently returned from Vienna, where she triumphed as the European Champion Lady Jockey and she'd made her decision to retire from race riding. Acting as a part-time teacher for West Oxfordshire College and doing guest-speaking at the races, Kelly was now ready to focus on another meaningful career.

We had reached an agreement that Kelly would become my first authorized instructor and conduct courses at West Oxfordshire College. I was absolutely convinced that if she gave it her best effort Kelly would become a leader in disseminating my concepts globally.

Kelly had mastered the art of riding horses, was well-educated and technically literate for 1995 standards but she was far more interested in hands-on work with horses and people.

Offices and paperwork just didn't seem to fit in to what Kelly saw as a fulfilling career.

We were having a discussion about an upcoming tour when I asked Kelly if she would kindly type a letter for me. She agreed and we sat in her father's office as she quite competently completed a two-page letter on an old typewriter that looked like it had come from a garage sale.

At the conclusion she made some suggestions on word changes that seemed quite impressive to me. I recall I felt Kelly had a good sense of communication and, for a horse girl, a high level of skills in an office environment. When the letter was finished I asked Kelly if she could loan me a stapler to put the two pages together.

With that Kelly reached into a drawer and produced the only stapler available. It was to be held between the thumb and index finger and if you filled it to the brim it would contain 10 staples. That stapler and the old typewriter constituted the sum total of the office equipment. "What is this?" I enquired and she informed me that it was a perfectly good stapler and adequate for the task.

Realizing that I was agreeing to put Kelly in charge of my UK business I was immediately concerned and we had a discussion about the need for Kelly to acquire things like a computer, maybe a fax machine and at the very least a decent stapler. I even offered to go to a store and get Kelly a workable stapler immediately, but she declined and was very quick to set me straight regarding her life's philosophies. She told me she didn't want too many THINGS in her life. She went on to explain that she felt that too many people made material objects all-important, they became slaves to them, which wasn't her style at all. The things that she was willing to make important were the horses and people to be helped, and her friends and her dog. She said she didn't want a bigger stapler because it was a sure step to starting a materialistic lifestyle.

Who am I to give advice to the contrary? I can't type, I've never copied anything, nor have I sent a fax. Life and those things that live and breathe consume 100 percent of me, but this means that I need someone around me who can fill in the gapsthose missing links so important in the modern world.

I explained these things to Kelly and once she saw how it fitted into her goals she soon made some life-changing decisions; and while the hands-on work was still her main interest she compromised and steadily began to build an organization that leads the rest of the world in the necessary aspects of running an international business.

I watched the confidence rise in Kelly as she took the time to read business books and she took advice on running computers and an office. Her ability to adjust to the modern world has produced an organization that has certainly made one old Californian cowboy very proud.

For the past 8 years or so Kelly has headed a team that has produced successful tours twice per year, her office now has 6 computers, and she has a team of wonderful people ready to answer questions from horse owners who wish to know how best to help their horses. You will even find a fax machine, a copier and a fantastic electronic stapler that doesn't even require you to press it!

I would never demand that my students do anything that they don't want to do. Making a decision, however, to give up certain things in one part of your life, to focus on success, is an admirable attribute. Kelly Marks made that kind of decision and now has the best of both worlds: her horses and students, as well as a business that is dedicated to making the world a better place for horses and people.

MONTY ROBERTS

CHAPTER ONE

The journey begins

OVERCOMING FEAR, GAINING CONFIDENCE
AND ACHIEVING SUCCESS WITH HORSES

Isn't it exciting? This is where it all starts!

I'd like to reveal an extraordinary fact about this book—it actually really does work! Can you believe that? I suppose as the author I shouldn't sound so surprised. I was always planning to give this book my best effort, tell a few anecdotes, suggest a few exercises that have worked for students and myself in the past. "That'll be fine," I thought. I had no intention of delving into my own present-day confidence issues. If someone had suggested I look into my own fear of driving a large horse trailer down a public highway as a part of the project, it might have shut down this "confidence book" idea altogether!

Yet in the course of writing it came to my attention that there were still a few confidence issues that I had pushed to one side, and it was time to take some action. As far as the horse trailer issue was concerned, once I had tackled this problem I actually got to the stage where I *wanted* to drive the horse trailer. Having seen myself as a "non-cook" my whole life, because of a change of attitude while researching this book I suddenly realized I was enjoying having people round for dinner. The "What do I really love to do?" exercises also helped me recognize that, although I retired from the competitive world over 10 years ago and haven't had "enough time" to give public demonstrations of my work recently, I felt I ought to make time now—after all, life isn't a dress rehearsal!

You may have bought this book to spur you on to pursue your dreams, or maybe because you are sometimes apprehensive when you're around horses and you'd like to deal with that. Or perhaps it's a bit of both? First

◁ *Dreams have no limit – go further.*

of all I would like to say a big "well done" for acknowledging that things could be better and for making the decision to do something about it.

There are hundreds, if not thousands, of less-than-confident riders out there. By admitting that there are ways in which you'd like to improve, you're taking responsibility (always a great start) and you can begin to do something positive to conquer your fears in the safest and fairest way—both to you and the horses with whom you are involved. This approach is much better than blaming your horse for being "nervy" and prone to balking, or punishing him for not being "genuine" and refusing jumps or getting nervous himself. You can breathe a sigh of relief now (go on, it's good for you), you are on your way to a more relaxed, yet intelligent and fun, way of being with horses.

Remember this book is written for YOU—whether you're studying for your finals in an equine degree or if you couldn't tell a hock from a withers. Whether you'd love to compete your own horse successfully, or if success to you is to dare even to *think* you might get to own a horse one day. Whether you get goosebumps when you dream of being picked to represent your country, or a chill goes down your spine when you think about trail riding on your own tomorrow.

If you think you're at a time in your life when you'd like to make some changes (and you could be 8 or 80 years old, it doesn't matter to me), then I'm ready, willing and able to work with you as your coach throughout this book. We'll work out what you'd like to change, where we should start and how best to go about seeing it through until we get the results you want.

To get the success you deserve we'll need to take a good look at all the things you're doing at the moment that are working in your favor (and make sure that you congratulate yourself on those), and then also all those (slightly weird) things that you're doing that really aren't helping you at all.

We want to make sure that you're enjoying yourself when you spend time around horses; after all, it's an expensive way to be miserable. And there's even more good news: there'll be no extra charge if you learn things in this book which will give you more freedom of choice and a sense of satisfaction in every area of your life!

I've designed this book so that purely the act of reading it will precipitate a fair number of positive results. (Make sure you note them down, because I'll be explaining later how you can get more of what you focus on.) You'll get even better results, though, if you could treat this book and yourself as a "work in progress." As with anything worthwhile, putting in the work is what will give you the best results. Do you think you can be disciplined enough to follow through? Discipline means finding ways to do what you say you're going to do, not finding excuses not to do it.

With this in mind, I've given you various assignments to complete as you read this book. On the next page is your first:

▽ *"A horse is worth more than riches."*
Spanish proverb

ASSIGNMENT
The story of your life

Right now, think of the person you want to be in 6 months' time. If your life were a film, who would play you? What lovely things do people say about you? How are you dressed? What fabulous things are you doing? This fantasized you may be nearer the "real" you than the person you portray now. Get to know the real you.

If your life were a film, how would you like to be cast? As the heroine – or the victim?

At times you might read something or do an exercise that makes you feel quite uncomfortable – this is often a good sign and the very time that you should press on and explore further. It may be that you feel you need one-to-one guidance, in which case you may want to find a qualified counselor through your doctor, or you can look at our website for more horse-related help.

I'm sorry if at any time you don't feel I'm being sympathetic enough to the reasons for your issues. I'd like you to understand that it's because I respect you and think you're a perfectly capable human being. While there are people who might prefer you to "stay in your place," I'm not one of them: I'm not prepared to lie to you and say, "Ah, poor little thing, you can't expect to achieve what you want because something happened in your past and now you'll always be one of those unlucky/victim-type people and you can never change…" Be honest, though, you wouldn't really *want* me to say that, would you? Feel the excitement of the changes you're going to make, keep picturing the fabulous new you. Admit it, isn't this going to be *so* worth it?

What does success actually mean to you?

You might think this book is slightly different to my previous books, which were far more about how you can make changes with your horses. In fact, this book might make the greatest impact of all on your work with horses.

If it weren't for the success of *Teach Your Horse Perfect Manners* and *Become Perfect Partners,* I certainly wouldn't have gone on to write about confidence. Being British, naturally I find it hugely embarrassing to describe anything I've done as "successful." So if I can, I'll qualify this immediately and explain my personal definition of success. It certainly isn't about being able to retire to some remote island in the Caribbean. However, the day I received an email with the subject line "Your book saved my life," I felt all my Christmases had come at once.

As a writer this comment is everything I'd dreamt about, and more. The sender explained that, because she had taught her horse the exercises in *Teach Your Horse Perfect Manners,* she had been able to get herself and her horse out of a really dangerous situation. Another touching email came from a young girl who had read *Teach Your Horse Perfect Manners* during Hurricane Katrina. She said, "I'm really pleased your book was with me (however wet it got) and it helped me a lot. After the hurricane, 10 of our 15 mini horses survived, but they were very traumatized by the experience. Your book helped me get their personalities back. Thank you so much." When I get messages like that it makes all my work worthwhile.

I'm writing this book with the intention of helping you make valuable changes to your life. When you've read it and worked through the exercises, please do drop me a line on how things are going, I just love hearing about your results!

The first steps

So, here I am, "an author," and although I'd always thought how amazing it would be to publish my own book one day, I wasn't born an author any more than I was born a rider, horse handler or teacher. I gained the confidence to write this book through successful experiences writing my other books. I gained the confidence to write those books because I had successful experiences writing short magazine articles; and I'm quite sure that I gained the confidence and discipline to write magazine articles from the continuing momentum I got from writing in my diary every day. It's a simple example of the saying, "Success breeds success."

So by these actions we've already got some key components of confidence—and these work for horses and people too:

1. Decide on your goal.
2. Start small.
3. Have the discipline to work on your goal regularly (daily, if possible).
4. Build on each success.
5. Keep on going!

▽ *We've all got to start somewhere...*

Coach Kelly's qualifications

Now if you're the skeptical type (which is fine), although secretly excited, you may feel you have to ask, "So, I'm thinking of appointing you as my coach, but what are your qualifications to teach me about gaining confidence? Not to mention the 'overcoming your fear and achieving success with horses' bit? Are you a qualified psychoanalyst? A qualified psychotherapist? Or are you just so massively confident yourself that you have never given a thought to anyone questioning your credentials?"

Err, nope, none of the above. In fact, I'm approaching it from the angle of "you teach what you need to learn." I don't think I could be nearly as helpful to you if I was just writing from the point of view, "I grew up incredibly talented and then went on to be a great success. Blah blah blah..." What I can tell you is that I was determined to live a life that involved horses (however impossible it seemed at times) and I don't know of anyone who has had more fun and satisfaction from horses throughout their life. I've always appreciated how lucky I am that amazing people have seemingly appeared from nowhere to help me along the way.

And yet, I understand now what an enormous privilege it is to be in a position to help others myself. There is such a feeling of pride when I see former students go on to do great things in their own right, and so while I can claim I wrote this book so I could "give something back," it's not really such an altruistic act after all. In fact, I believe it's another important part of the same journey that started all those years ago.

I really appreciate your picking up this book, and I appreciate that when you're not sure in which direction life is heading it can feel lonely and worrying. If only I'd believed the people who told me that it was all going to work out in the end! We can often feel isolated with our different concerns and confidence issues, and yet there are so many people who feel just the way you might feel now.

Sometimes when you lack confidence life feels like you've come into the classroom late and everyone except you knows the rules and what they're supposed to be doing. It can make you susceptible to bullying (however subtle) and soon you start to doubt yourself more and more.

Working with me, you're listening to a person who has been there, done that, bought the T-shirt but, most importantly, is on your side. Now we can work together so that in no time at all *you* will be the one saying to people,

"Yes, I know exactly how you feel. In fact, would you believe that I used to lack confidence? (No, really?!) But what I found is that if you…"

My journey with horses

Anyway, let me tell you how it all started for me—and how I learnt, far too slowly…

The cleanest child in Berkshire

My horsey career didn't get off to the brightest start: severe head injuries at the age of 6 (it wasn't considered important to wear hard hats in those days) made it look as if I wouldn't live to my next birthday, never mind ride again. When I finally got my own pony at the ripe old age of 11 (I thought it was never going to happen) and realized that I could achieve my life's ambition of competing at a show, I found I was shaking and actually physically sick.

You might have sympathy for me and think, "Well, she was just a young girl and sometimes those jumping or event classes can be pretty scary." But what I haven't told you yet is which class it was that had me racked with pain and in pieces mentally—it was "The Best-Turned Out" class. All my pony Seamus and I had to do was walk round in one direction and keep clean for 20 minutes. You'd have thought I was at least going for a Puissance wall at 7 feet 4 inches, or that all my country's hopes rested on my getting a clear round for the Olympic gold!

Choose a good-quality label

However, nothing deterred me for one moment from pursuing my dream as the cleanest child and pony in Berkshire. I've heard people call children "nervous," when in fact they were showing much lesser signs of anxiety than I did. And perhaps those children go on from being "nervous children" to "nervous adults." Of course, at that time I didn't understand that the label you put on feelings is the important thing. Luckily I never used the label "nerves" to describe how I felt. I just thought it was excitement that I was feeling, because it was, for me, such an incredibly thrilling and important experience, and with no one telling me any different, I continued to think this way.

This line of thinking was just as well, because once you give yourself a label it can so easily become part of your self-image and your idea of "who you are," so then your mind will find ways to "prove" it. For instance, if a dog jumps out of a hedge and my horse and I both jump 3 feet in the air, my natural instinct is to mutter, "Stupid dog!" and think no more of it. Whereas someone who has allowed themselves to become tagged with the "nervous" label will revert to their default, "Oh, that's typical. Look at me! I shouldn't have been shocked like that. My heart's beating really fast now. That's because I'm a nervous rider. Oh dear, oh dear..."

It's so important to realize that each one of us has the ability to choose how we will react in any given situation. When we can't control events, at least we can still take control of what we tell ourselves about what happened.

Growing ambition

As I grew in ability (i.e. I could steer round the ring right *and* left, mostly stay on top of my pony, etc.) and my aspirations soared from merely being clean to jumping obstacles as well, my ambition was to become the British jumper rider, Marion Coakes. However, in order for that to happen (we can discuss patently unrealistic ambitions—such as transmogrification—

later on in the book), I realized that there was something about my *attitude* that I had to change. Curiously, I found some books around the house at that time; a very old book on hypnotism and another book called *A Lazy Man's Way to Riches*, which was basically about setting goals. Perhaps they were quite heavy books for an 11-year-old to be reading, but I devoured them as if they were new Harry Potter novels. How exciting to be able to create your own destiny! Definitely magic!

During the course of this book I want to tell you some stories and I want them to seep into your brain so that you gradually believe that they're *your* stories. With this subtle brainwashing* working on your subconscious, along with very practical ideas, you'll exclaim, "How obvious! Why didn't I think of that before?" (Or if you did think of it before, you'll wonder why you haven't been consistently doing it.) Suddenly you'll find you *want* to ride that horse, take that job or take positive action against bullying. You will develop a different perspective on things, it will become clear to you that you really can make a difference.

It's always comforting to know that others have trodden the same path as the one that you are perhaps on now. They've experienced the same fears and insecurities and they have come through them successfully, which means there is no reason why you can't too. Only a very small percentage of people ever take the time to think through their dreams, never mind actively devising a plan of how to achieve them. So just by following through, you're already 95 percent of the way there.

And that means you can achieve your dreams, too. I know for a fact that you're in the top 10 percent of the "most likely to succeed" class. After all, how many other people do you know who care enough to buy a book about achieving dreams? You could steal even more of a lead if having read it, you take immediate action!

"Success" is something most people in the United States strive for. What we need to remember are those who astonish us by always pushing

---

* I guess I ought to confess now, I actually did train as a hypnotist in the 1980s – but I only use it for good, in a female Robin Hood sort of a way. It's not something I generally make known as it can make some people nervous, but just watch the pendulum now and say to yourself, "I trust Kelly and I am no longer afraid, I trust Kelly and I am no longer afraid..." (Most useful of all I can teach you to hypnotize *yourself*, which is a really helpful tool.)

Friendship is born at the moment when one person says to another, "What, you too? I thought I was the only one."

C. S. LEWIS

the limits—perhap failing as they test their comfort zone. Such individuals are heroes precisely because of how well they *fail.* However, they will remain heroes to those of us who have ever taken a chance in life, and who don't think life is a spectator sport but make a decision to get out there and "have a go" instead. At least if we fail, *we fail while daring greatly* (Theodore Roosevelt).

Don't ask what the world needs—ask what makes you come alive and go and do that. Because what the world needs is people who have come alive.

HOWARD THURMAN

"Not good enough to clean his shoes!"

In the summer of 1995 I would never have believed that I'd be riding horses in California for Monty Roberts, or that one day I would be training my own horses in France. At that time my life was a mess: I had just split up with my wife and was out of work. My life was empty and seemed pointless.

I was sitting in my bedroom looking for an answer, racking my brains. I made a pot of coffee and turned on the TV. The program on television was about a man who talked to horses. I sat mesmerized as I watched Monty Roberts training horses, and I could not believe what I was seeing. I started to think, "I wonder if there's any way I could learn the methods he uses?" I didn't sleep well that night. Horses were going round and round in my head.

I went to my local bar at lunchtime to meet some friends and told them what I had seen. I heard about 100 verses of "Dr. Doolittle" as my friends laughed at me. As they merrily progressed to "Champion the Wonder Horse" an old man walked in. At that moment the Olympics were on the TV in the bar and British ski jumper Eddie "the Eagle" Edwards was about to make his jump. We all watched him at the top of the ramp as he pulled down his goggles, leant backwards and then launched himself. He flew up into the air, landed on his head and sprawled down the slope like a starfish. We "boys" exploded into laughter, beer spraying from our mouths.

I'd seen the quiet old man before and he'd always kept to himself—but not today. He jumped up in front of the TV and shouted, "How dare you laugh at that man! You come in here drinking beer half the day, thinking you are wonderful. Which one of you has ever done something to be proud of like him? Last week he was a construction worker, this week he's representing his country at the Olympics. He set out to achieve his dream and he's done it. He's a true winner. Not one of you is good enough to clean his shoes!"

Five of us wild men of the area were trying to hide behind a pint glass. We were all so truly humbled you could hear a pin drop. He was right and I knew it. That old man and Eddie Edwards were just the inspiration I needed to make my dreams become a reality.

JOHN MAGUIRE, HORSEMAN AND DREAMER

Certainly we've all suffered setbacks in the past, but from now on we're going to view every experience as a chance for personal upliftment, learning and growth. So it's onwards and upwards for us. I want you to relax now, but also to concentrate. I'd also like you to take any of my and others' experiences that turned out well and realize you make them part of your experience too. I want you to enter a world where the very best can happen; where plans will work out; where good overcomes evil and where dreams really do come true. Enjoy.

▽ *"The difference between the impossible and the possible lies in a person's determination."*
Tommy Lasorda

Small goals—it's the little things that count

When I was asked by Kelly to relate a story that pointed out the value of confidence, the first one I mentioned was that of George Apple (name changed). While it's true my life has been filled with stories that show the value of confidence, this one probably heads the list.

George's father was working as a farmer's butcher: he would come to your property, slaughter a steer, sheep or hog, then take it to his facility and process it for your freezer. George's dad was a rough sort of guy. We would term him a "redneck" in America—hard-drinking, hard-playing; he was often making the round of bars with George's mother.

On this particular day in the early 1970s the butcher brought along his son, 13-year-old George. Smallish and handsome, he was an outgoing young man expressing great energy. The problem was that most of his energy was negative. He seemed to be quite angry at the world as I engaged him in conversation, and I discovered that he was in great trouble with the law at that time. Young George had a date with the court to determine whether he could remain with his parents or would have to be institutionalized.

After a conversation with his dad I agreed to meet with the judge and see if we could work out a plan to assist young George. I was told that he was quite interested in learning how to ride horses and was an ambitious worker. I was also told that he hated school and any form of authority. I think his dad used the phrase "free spirit."

The meeting with the juvenile court judge revealed many aspects that I was unaware of. The dad was a drug addict and the mother was engaged in activities that no mother has a right to expose her children to. George was in trouble, but the family was in even greater disarray.

The judge agreed that if I were to take George on as a foster son, see to his needs and encourage a decent education he would legally sign him over to me. The parents agreed and my family was larger by one 13-year-old at the stroke of a pen.

When George arrived, possessions in hand, the first thing that he said to me was, "Hey, turkey, what are you doing? And what do you want from me?" I stopped short, thought for a minute and said, "I want you to respect me, but I want to earn your respect. So until I do, go ahead and call me turkey, but when I've earned your respect I want you to call me Mr. Roberts."

We had some serious sessions for the next two weeks or so. I put my concepts into place, created contracts with George and attempted to give him respect, love and positive

▷ *Monty Roberts with children. "The good teacher explains. The superior teacher demonstrates. The best teacher inspires." William A. Ward*

consequences each time he seemed to get things right. We had our highs and our lows, but progress was apparent.

It seems as though it was around 2 to 3 weeks later, when George was completing a relatively successful day, that he walked up to me briskly, looked me in the eye and stuck out his hand. I grasped his hand firmly and while I was shaking it I heard those words I'll never forget: "Mr. Roberts."

One might ask at this point what I did, specifically, that altered this young man's behavior so dramatically. First of all I conversed with George about the setting of goals for his life. We started with some very basic aims he had. I agreed to help him meet these early elements, providing that he would meet requirements that I set for him. I dealt with the small things like language and table manners, and his clothing. It certainly also included the basic elements of caring for the horses he was dealing with. He now had an ambition to become a trainer's stable foreman, which would require him to speak Spanish really well. I observed as he practiced the language, gradually becoming fluent, and having conversations with the Mexican grooms and stall-muckers on the farm. From that point forward I watched George get his life on the right track more and more with each day. I watched his school grades sky rocket as he became more interested in an academic education. I witnessed George become the best stall-mucker on Flag Is Up farms,

laughing at those that took 15 to 20 minutes to do what he could do in just 3 to 5 minutes.

George was growing out of his job as an exercise rider of thoroughbred racehorses. His confidence soared as I encouraged him to become a very productive member of his school football team, wrestling team and even gymnastics.

While George was an excellent rider and an outstanding athlete, he was also becoming very interested in succeeding in some form of business. In the horse business, I think we would say, "he's getting the bit between his teeth." In one of our conversations George told me of an uncle who was manufacturing furniture, mainly chairs. He said that his uncle's plant employed mostly Spanish-speaking Mexicans. George was now 19, with a diploma in business administration. He wanted a chance to assist his uncle by becoming a shop foreman. He would guide the efforts of about 40 fabricators (workers) in their furniture manufacturing effort. I was quick to agree to the idea and George went off to Los Angeles filled with confidence.

As I recall, about 3 months later George came to me saying he had recommended to his uncle that he be allowed to explore the possibility of opening a plant in Tijuana, Mexico, just over the border south of San Diego, California.

George indicated that he felt he could save half the manufacturing costs with his idea. His fluency in Spanish worked well for him and he sailed into business with his uncle in Tijuana.

At this point in the story I think it's important to remind the reader that when young George first came to me he was a very angry young man. He told me many times about how he hated what his parents were doing. One should remember that he was at prison's doorstep and was clearly heading down a path straight into a life of crime. In those first weeks if you had have asked me what George's levels of confidence were as to becoming a successful, productive adult, I would have said zero.

After approximately one year it was evident George's efforts would save the company about 40 percent of their initial cost of merchandise. George's agreement with his uncle was now earning him about 4 times his original salary. When the uncle realized how well George was doing he demanded they renogotiate their agreement. George came to me immediately for advice. Obviously I was angry with what the uncle was doing, but George had a plan.

He told me he would like to go into business for himself. He said he needed help but he felt the clients he had serviced would go with him. I agreed to give George the help he required, and soon he was the owner of his own company.

George was quickly a flying success in the chair manufacturing business in the US. He remained in Mexico with his plant for about 2 years and then moved it into California for a more stable political environment. The clients stayed with him and his output grew like crazy.

As George brought his business back to the US he announced to me that he planned to marry. He asked me to be a part of the marriage ceremony and my son, Marty, was his best man. They were as close as two brothers could be and George as close to me as a son could possibly be. George's father died of an overdose very near the time of the wedding and his mother was nowhere to be seen.

With confidence levels as high as anyone can imagine, this young man has used his early opportunities to create a wonderful family, now with 3 children and a business that operates at the level of a 26 million-dollar income in 2005. George recently told me that he had at least some of his chairs in every major hotel in Las Vegas, Nevada.

It is incredible what human beings can do if given the opportunity to see positive consequences for positive actions. While it is important that they pay a price for negative actions, it is the achievements that generate the levels of confidence necessary for a breakthrough performance.

George Apple exemplifies the psychological phenomenon of learning how to have fun getting it right; and horses played a major role in the early development of this ultra-successful businessman.

MONTY ROBERTS

THE ARENA

It is not the critic who counts: not the man who points out how the strong man stumbles, or where the doer of deeds could have done better. The credit belongs to the man or woman who is actually in the arena, whose face is marred by dust and sweat and blood: who strive valiantly; who err and come short again and again, because there is no effort without error and shortcomings; but those who actually strive to do the deeds; who know the great enthusiasms, the great devotions; who spend themselves in a worthy cause; who at the best know in the end the triumph of high achievement, and who at worst, if they fail, at least fail while daring greatly, so that their place shall never be with those cold and timid souls who know neither victory nor defeat.

THEODORE ROOSEVELT

address at the Sorbonne, Paris, 23rd April 1910

CHAPTER TWO

Perfectly valid fears

AND GOOD REASONS FOR LACK OF CONFIDENCE

Let's take a moment to assess the situation before we leap into the "arena," start throwing ourselves down ski slopes in the Olympics or hire a horse to go hunting. It's time for a quick reality check. This isn't intended to limit your ambitions and dreams, but to look a little at how your situation might suggest the best way to proceed. If you're a novice rider, say, with only 2 months of lessons under your belt, and someone offers you her dressage stallion (which they describe as "temperamental") to exercise while her broken leg recovers, you're not failing to be bold and live life to the full if you decline the offer. You're simply making it more likely that you get the chance to lead a long and fulfilling life.

Perhaps you'll decide to spend quite a lot of that life becoming the sort of rider who will relish—and cope with—such a challenge. However, the real question is, when is it reasonable to be concerned for your safety and take sensible precautions; and when does fear become debilitating and prevent you from enjoying life?

A friend of mine, who had a phobia of spiders, saw a hypnotherapist who successfully treated her. Afterwards, her mother decided to go to the same therapist to overcome her fear of flying. "I'm sorry, I really can't help you," the therapist told her, "because that's a perfectly valid fear!" It's unfortunate, perhaps, to come across a therapist who is as doubtful about flying as you are, but it isn't essential for this lady to take plane trips, and so she has settled quite happily on summer holidays in Scotland and taking the train to Europe.

In the same way, I don't think anyone can say that we *have* to ride horses: it is a choice that we make after carefully weighing up the pros and

◁ *"If you want to conquer fear, don't sit at home and think about it. Go out and get busy." Andrew Carnegie*

cons of the sport. The fact is, it certainly isn't a hobby without some risks and it would be irresponsible to encourage a nervous person to ride simply by saying, "Take this nerve tonic and everything will be fine."

My friend's mother might have fared better by seeing a statistician rather than a flight-phobic hypnotherapist. If you are concerned about the safety of a situation, then the facts can help us reach an informed decision about whether the risks are acceptable to us or not. For instance, one could point out that Virgin Atlantic haven't had an accident since they began flying passengers in 1982. And, in fact, there are many airlines that have never had a fatality or accident connected with them, just as there are many riding establishments or branches of horsemanship where accidents are extremely rare. It doesn't mean that accidents are impossible; it just "lowers the odds," as gamblers say.

▽ *It's always a sensible idea to weigh the risks of chosen activities before you agree to take part in them.*

Avoidable and unavoidable accidents

While we should be aware that freak accidents do occur (you'd be surprised how many people are admitted to the hospital each year after having an accident involving a household air freshener), there are also certain things that people do that are clearly ridiculous. It is probably not politically correct to describe people as "asking for trouble", however, there are, without doubt, people who do exactly this and you don't want to be one of them. You can even win a posthumous award for the most idiotic way of bringing about your own death. The Darwin Awards, named in honor of Charles Darwin, the father of evolution, commemorate those who improve our gene pool by removing themselves from it through utter brainlessness. It's worth taking a peek at www.darwinawards.com to get some tips on avoidable accidents, such as why it's not a good idea to train a dog to "fetch" when you throw lighted dynamite, or to use an artillery shell as a desk paperweight.

We know that the difference between intelligent people and stupid people is no more complicated than that intelligent people do intelligent things and stupid people do stupid things. We need to be ever vigilant that we're getting these two things the right way round. The quickest way to destroy your own confidence is to do a lot of silly things that have very negative outcomes. Conversely, the best way to build confidence is to have as many successful experiences as possible – and that's what we're examining in this chapter.

Prevention is better than cure

In the early part of our lives it is the duty of our parents, or at least of the adults around us, to protect us, because as children we have no concept of danger. Of course, it's best not to have to learn from experience (as I did) that riding (or, more accurately, falling off) without a hard hat can cause a nasty head injury; or, as others have learned, that taking a bucket of food into a strange group of horses is dangerous because you stand the risk of getting crowded, knocked over or kicked.

As we grow into and (if we're lucky) reach adulthood we greatly benefit from experienced people helping us to evaluate different situations. That's why gaining as much beneficial experience and getting a good education in the subject of your choice—whether it's in the form of lessons, books or just hanging around knowledgeable people to watch their every move and pester them with questions—is invaluable when it comes to making a sensible assessment of a situation.

However, this carries with it a small warning: if someone tells you something that really doesn't "feel" right to you, on asking a lot more questions, don't hold back on going somewhere different or seeking a second opinion – or even a third or a fourth. Whatever information you're given should make sense to you. I've lost count of the number of people I've met at clinics who have come along because they've been told by "everyone at their barn" that their horse "just needs a good smack." The student usually says something along the lines of, "The problem is that they're experienced and I'm not, but it doesn't make a lot of sense. I don't understand why I should hit my horse when he is frightened." There are usually other students listening to this, nodding in agreement because they've had the same experience. But I'm happy to say that at our Intelligent Horsemanship clinics we can show people a kinder and more effective way for them to solve their problems with their horses, by using methods with which they feel entirely comfortable. This is what makes teaching so rewarding.

At our Intelligent Horsemanship clinics we have a certain number of students who are generally apprehensive about handling horses. By the time they leave us, they will be far more self-assured in dealing with their animals. I hasten to add that this isn't because we've encouraged any "gung-ho" bravery or played them stirring music so that they go away psyched-up and ready to "feel the fear and do it anyway." (I'm not denying that these methods do also have their place, and we'll discuss this later.)

The fact of the matter is that a little caution in the beginning can often pay dividends later. Students will go away more confident because they have learnt that it makes real sense to be careful and cautious around horses – particularly when approaching an unfamiliar animal – and will learn how to read signals from the horse and move around him in such a way as to put themselves at minimum risk.

I generally find that it is the people who come to horses later in life who put themselves in the most danger. Pony clubs and riding schools can be wonderful for drilling those little, yet so important, points into a young

△ Never be complacent
around horses. Always go
into situations knowing
what to expect.

person's head, such as "Check your girth," "Turn your pony's head toward you at the gate before turning him out," "Make sure the pony knows where you are." Lessons learned while very young will translate into second nature later in life, but if you've missed out on those early lessons (or if you have been taught the wrong ones) it's never too late to learn the vital points.

This is what the students on our courses are doing—they are beginning to acquire the skills they need in order to be safe around horses. This is one of the most critical points of this entire book: a common reason for people to lack confidence is that they don't have the physical, emotional and mental skills they need in order to do the job well.

How to kill confidence

In my previous books I explained how we could teach our horses to buck, rear—and basically be bad—so that we can study the process and then turn it around. We can do exactly the same thing with human emotions such as depression and lack of confidence.

For instance, here's a sure-fire way to spend a day feeling depressed: spend a night drinking as much alcohol as possible. Make sure you wake up in the filthiest surroundings, then don't wash or get any fresh air. Put on some really downbeat music and watch the most miserable soaps you can find on television (ideally last year's repeat), or one of the Christmas

ASSIGNMENT
Thinking things through

I'd like you to recall a time when you could have thought things through more successfully. Write down the main mistakes you made and how you would do it differently in future. Doing this exercise will help to act as a memory jog next time you're about to do something stupid. Also, if your answer is "I don't know," that could be the very reason that the mistake is sticking in your mind. Your subconscious wants you to figure it out!

The only real mistake is the one from which we learn nothing.

JOHN POWELL

episodes—they're generally good for a suicide or two, or a marriage break down, or just lots of doom and crying). Make sure that you don't have anything decent to eat in the house—half a can of your most hated food that looks like it's going bad will do. The only human contact you are allowed is with people you dislike and who dislike you (and, preferably, who are also depressed themselves). Try to concentrate on all the bad things that have happened in your life, all the times people have let you down, all the things you've tried and failed to do. Make sure that even your successes are seen in a bad light, and convince yourself that they were all flukes anyway. If a cheerful thought comes into your head, then banish it immediately. If you can drum up any remaining energy, try to think of something sad.

Great! So now we've warmed up with feeling depressed, let's see how we can work on our confidence. For those of you who haven't been concentrating, we'll start by developing our *lack* of confidence. Let's assume we want to lose our confidence in riding. First of all, take as long a break as possible from riding (after all, the more frequently we do something successfully the more confident we're going to get, and we don't what *that* to happen). Get yourself in the right frame of mind by watching a "thrills and spills" video, and replay the most crashing falls frame by frame. Envisage yourself in those situations and focus on your anxiety until you begin to get palpitations. (Incidentally, the first and only time I watched a film like this was when I worked at an equine college and was told to show it to the students as "light entertainment." That's a bit like your in-flight film being *Aircrash at Death Valley* or showing *Jaws* to a group of surfers.)

Be as physically unfit as possible. (If you could be suffering from something that affects your balance, that would be especially good, or perhaps a sprain, a heavy dose of flu, or an ear infection.) The horse you are going to ride should be spooky and fresh, and its tack totally uncomfortable for both of you. (A little flat hunt seat saddle would be ideal.) The horse, preferably completely unknown to you, should be physically difficult for you to ride, i.e. 17.3hh, and so wide you can't get your legs around him. Don't spend any time with the horse, just jump on and go off on a ride with the most inconsiderate group of people you can find, who will gallop off repeatedly without waiting for you if you get left behind and your horse is clearly getting upset. Fall off.

Let's get serious with some straight-talking advice, because I really do care

In my previous books, *Teach Your Horse Perfect Manners* and *Become Perfect Partners*, I concentrated on how to improve your relationship with your horse, both on the ground and when riding. Please read those books to ensure that your horse is not being blamed for problems that are not of his making. However, in this book I am making YOU (or your child) a priority, rather than your horse or pony. Yes, you have read that correctly. If you or your child are consistently being hurt by a horse or pony then I want you to imagine me sitting there right now, with a rather grim look on my face, saying, "Please sit down. We need to talk."

It never ceases to amaze me how many people ride horses that are patently dangerous, and continue to do so (frequently injuring themselves) even though they are deriving no enjoyment whatsoever from riding. They often treat the experience as though it's an ordeal that they must endure to repent for some sin or other. In the Middle Ages hair shirts were terrible garments made from goats' hair that were worn in the form of a shirt or as a girdle around the loins "by way of mortification and penance." Nowadays it seems more fashionable to use a dysfunctional relationship with a human or animal (sometimes both) to make one's life completely and utterly miserable.

Personally, though, I'm not a fan of unnecessary suffering for animals *or* people. It's true that we must work out what our duty is towards our animals (which is why you should think *very carefully* before committing to buying a horse or pony and even more carefully before breeding one); however, people do make mistakes.

If you have made the mistake of buying a horse that is extremely dangerous for you, you have to have the courage and strength of character to make a sensible decision as to what to do next. It may be that you have to pay for the horse to be re-trained so that you can sell him on honestly or, possibly, if the training goes really well, you may even be able to keep him for yourself. Perhaps someone more experienced will buy him from you at a much reduced price, and so you might make a financial loss. If your horse is not rideable but is safe to handle, you may just want to keep him – as long as he's happy, healthy and has some company, there's no need to feel guilty about him not "having a job" if he clearly dislikes being ridden. Although I think there are lots of horses that enjoy being ridden, I also think that quite a few wouldn't be bothered if no one sat on them again. You might still get an enormous amount of pleasure out of simply having him around. Again, it's all about making choices, and there's no law that says you have to ride your horse.

Be a careful parent around horses

Although for an adult there may be a stoical aspect to a decision to go on enduring an unhappy situation, my personal opinion is that it isn't fair to have so little regard for the physical and emotional well-being of a child. Children rely on adults for their safety and protection.

△ *"Perfect" horses come in all shapes and sizes. Orion, here, is an Icelandic pony, and his owner clearly adores him.*

We all know there are certain risks to a child riding a pony, just as there are if they ride a bike or go skiing or take the bus alone. I'm not suggesting that we wrap children in cotton wool or remove all adventure from their lives. However, it's madness to buy a pony on impulse because you or your child "feels sorry" for a pony that has previously been abused, for example. The pony may well have pain issues that can never be resolved and now your child will be suffering the consequences. A horse-crazy child is going to fall in love with the first pony he or she is presented with, so responsible adults need to be kind but firm in directing a child's attention away from an unsuitable pony, just as they would if their 10-year-old daughter insisted she was "in love" with the local drug dealer.

If your child is being bullied by a pony or consistently dumped on the ground or run away with, this is not a suitable pony! You need to be aware that there are a great many pony breeds that are not suitable for children or novice owners. I won't mention a specific breed lest I get lynched by breeders and, to be fair, you can't really say, "Welsh ponies, particularly Welsh Section Ds, are much too hot for the average novice rider," or "Sport ponies are actually bred specifically for adults," because there are some lovely,

ASSIGNMENT
Thinking things through

Think carefully about your responsibilities before buying a horse. If the seller has lied to you and he's not a safe horse, would you be willing to lie to the next buyer, or perhaps go through a lengthy court case? You may be prepared to lose money, but supposing you grow fond of your horse and know that, by sending him to a sale, he could soon be passed from dealer to dealer – how would you feel about that? If he needs extra veterinary care or to go for extensive reschooling, do you have the finances available? If he had no useful purpose would you still be prepared to keep him for the rest of his life, or could you make the decision to have him put down? These are decisions that you will have to consider if you buy the wrong horse.

In dreams begins responsibility.

W.B. YEATS

manageable and quiet Welsh and Sport ponies around. However, if you are going for a specific breed, you might benefit by studying their bloodlines. There are stallions that are notorious (but only to those "in the know") for having extremely difficult offspring, but there are always enough novices to come along and buy them and therefore they continue to be bred.

Please don't break your child's heart (or your own) by buying a totally unsuitable animal, for the simple reason that there are also lots of perfectly delightful ponies around with whom the whole family can fall in love!

Save money by turning your child off horses for life! (With thanks to the www.intelligenthorsemanship.co.uk discussion group)

- Before your child is old enough to take an interest in anything equine, buy her an outrageously aggressive and dangerous pony (don't worry, this is quite legal) and allow her to be terrorized by him.
- When your child is very young, force him to walk round the cross-country course at Rolex and witness crashing falls.
- Make sure she is totally over-horsed and has no control whatsoever of the pony she is going to ride.
- Explain that riders can never be "fair-weather riders" and ensure he rides in the depths of winter for so long that he feels his fingers and toes might drop off.
- Force her to compete and then humiliate her in public when she doesn't win; in addition, convince her that she has just ruined your life.
- Non-horsey parents should act hysterically while the child is around a pony to ensure no fear is left untransmitted.
- Let the child ride her very first lesson in her sneakers (no socks) so that the stirrups keep getting stuck until her feet are black and blue.
- Laugh or shout at your child's incapacity to control the pony and tell him he has to fall off 100 times before he will ever make a rider.
- Continuously belittle your child and lead him to believe he will never be able to ride properly.
- Practice shouting loudly about how hopeless your child is. Ensure you have an audience for this – public humiliation always helps.
- Tell your child lots of horror stories about accidents (they don't have to be true, just gruesome).

Advice on buying a horse or pony

- Always take a trusted, experienced person with you.
- It's helpful if your companion videotapes the horse as you ride.
- The ideal horse or pony is one from your area that you have known about for ages. Look out for ponies about to be outgrown!
- Write out a list of questions to ask the seller. If you don't ask a specific question the seller isn't obliged to volunteer damaging information.
- Always have your horse or pony vetted; it's much better to know in advance if he has any physical issues. In a five-stage vetting, back problems can be missed, also arthritis and feet problems. Read the list of what's covered and, according to the age and career of the horse, you may want extra X-rays and blood tests (including a doping test).

Risk analysis

Although I know of many cases where affirmations, hypnotherapy and NLP (Neuro Linguistic Programming; more of this in chapter 5) techniques have been very helpful to people, *first of all* I believe we need to do an analysis of how valid your fears really are.

How safe are your riding experiences? What is it exactly that you fear the most—and what is the likelihood that it could happen? Although there are some accidents that come completely out of the blue, calculating the risk factor of each situation shouldn't be too difficult. For example, an experienced rider with a good seat, walking a quiet, aged horse round an indoor arena. Risk factor: 1 percent. A very inexperienced and unstable rider jumping a novice, unschooled, highly strung horse round a cross-country course on a wet and windy day. Risk factor: 99 percent.

Next time you are going out riding and you feel fear (as opposed to being excited by a competition, which is an entirely different thing), do a risk analysis of the situation. Let's say you are nervous of taking your horse on a three-mile ride on your own, on a route around the area where he is kept. Don't feel bad because you "shouldn't be" feeling nervous—maybe you should. What is it exactly that you think might happen? Is your horse prone to overexcitement when he's out in open spaces? If he did buck and kick would you be able to stay on? Are you worried about falling off and no-one knowing where you are?

Are you thinking of buying your child a pony?

I was so excited the first time I bought my daughter Daisy a pony. The woman who was selling the pony was lovely (I thought), so knowledgeable and sincere, and she convinced me that all she wanted was for Daisy to have a lovely time!

What I did not realize was that the poor pony was on steroids and as soon as she arrived at the barn where I'd arranged for her to stay she coughed as if with her last gasps. What I also failed to realize was that it would take a lawyer and six months to get my money back. The pony delivered to me was a dream, a beautiful gleaming chestnut with fabulous muscle. Without the illegal drugs, though, which were destroying her kidneys, the little pony fell apart until she was just a poor skinny little rabbit.

After the disappointment and emotional upheaval of that experience (if I could have afforded to I would have kept the pony because we felt so sorry for her!) we gave up any thought of ponies for nearly 5 years. But on deciding to take the plunge again it all seemed equally exciting. This time I made enquiries, spoke to the right people and had a five-stage vetting – so what could go wrong?

I must confess that the seller *did* mention that he could sometimes be "a little difficult to lead in a halter." However, after we'd bought him and when, every time Daisy took him out he pulled her over and dragged her through the mud, it didn't matter, as none of us wanted to lead him anyway! She did some little showing classes with him and every time she had to trot him for the judge I would hold my breath, wondering if he was just going to keep on going – I could imagine him cantering out of the ring with her determinedly holding the reins. He was described in his classified ad as a "fun pony for a child": it's interesting what different people's idea of fun is.

SANDRA O'HALLORAN

You win or lose the day you buy your horse.

OLD SAYING

Introducing children to ponies

Many adults admit to being afraid of horses, but fear is not inherited; it's more reactionary, and most of these adults will have had bad experiences with horses as children, such as being run away with, falling off, or being bitten or kicked.

It's a pity—and really quite surprising—that adults (often parents) who lack any knowledge of horses will often happily let their children wander into a pony's field unsupervised, or they insist on putting a child on a pony without first discovering his history and nature. So if the child falls off (which he or she invariably will), they might say, "Get back up again, it builds confidence!" I can recall watching small children at summer fairs who screamed their heads off as they were hoisted up for a pony ride by well-meaning parents.

Learning to ride properly is a time-consuming and practice-intensive exercise, and one that requires the skill of a qualified instructor. Children must start on a highly-trained horse or pony; it's so important at this formative stage in their lives. Anything less might lead to trouble, to potentially destroying their confidence and causing them some day in the future to relate a horror story of the time they were thrown from a horse on the local farm.

Starting a young rider should be no different to starting a young horse on its career path—you need to take slow, informed and patient steps to encourage the beginner towards success. Children who have received the best guidance and training are a delight to watch with their horse or pony. With a little forethought and planning, anyone's child can achieve their riding goals – be it on a social or professional level. As responsible adults we shouldn't jeopardize our children's potential through a couple of seconds of poor judgement.

JOHN WILLIAMS, AMERICAN HORSE BREEDER

ASSIGNMENT
Your personal risk analysis

Find a pen and paper and make a list of your concerns. Once you have set down your worries in black and white, you can put your mind to work on practical solutions that you can write down beside them.

The solutions may include: don't go on the ride for the time being, or keep having good-quality lessons with an understanding instructor so that your seat and riding position are so strong your confidence soars. If you are more confident with your horse while you are on the ground, then you might consider leading him round the ring (it'll make you fitter as well!).

Take sensible precautions that will make you feel safer while out riding—wear a body protector, have a neckstrap on your horse, take a cell phone with you (switched to silent!), and always tell someone where you are going and what time you are expecting to be back. You might also have to take a realistic look at your horse: is he too big for you too handle? Would an older, less highly-strung horse suit you better? Would he be perfectly all right if he perhaps had more turn out, less feed? Or does he really need a companion on rides?

There are two kinds of responses to the risks that you have identified. You can take action to prevent an accident happening, or you can take steps to prevent yourself, your horse, or anyone else, from being injured as a consequence. For example, if you know that your horse is very spooky when he hacks out alone, then one way of reducing the risk would be to hack out in company.

Don't forget that you should also wear a well-fitting riding hat—of course, it won't prevent an accident happening, but it will protect you from a head injury if you come off.

When you look at your list of solutions, make sure that you have identified ways of preventing the accident happening in the first place, as well as listing all the ways in which you can reduce the potential for someone or something getting hurt if things go wrong.

To improve at anything we have to come out of our comfort zone. However, it's wise for both horse and rider to work their way up in small steps. For instance, many people do have the odd fall jumping in the early days, particularly if they are working with a novice jumper, so it makes more sense to admit that this can happen and start your schooling in a ring with a nice, soft surface, rather than just pretending it could *never* happen.

People say I'm brave, but I'm not brave, I prepare every step of the way.
I walk the course three times and I visualize jumping successfully over
every jump. If I don't feel fully prepared, I won't jump.

ANDREW HOY AT BURGHLEY

Post-traumatic stress

Before we delve into the exciting world of developing your confidence, there is one more consideration you should be aware of. As I wrote this book I realized there might be some people who are reading this because their confidence has been shattered as a consequence of being in an accident: maybe it was one involving a horse, or perhaps some other kind of accident. Most people who have experienced such a traumatic event go through feelings of apprehension or nervousness for a while afterwards. However, for the most part, the horrors of the traumatic event will fade within a few weeks and these people should gradually start to feel more like their old selves.

It is possible, though, that as a result of an accident (especially one involving injuries or where there was a serious threat to their safety), the person can have a hard time letting go of the feelings of anxiety, fear or depression that might have followed. This is partly because there are areas of our brain whose job it is to record the feelings of fear that are associated with particular memories, and it can take time, effort and sometimes skilled help to enable this cellular memory to reprogram its response to certain events. For a very few people this can develop into Post-Traumatic Stress Disorder – you don't have to have been involved in a disaster or lived in a war zone to experience such a severe reaction. If you have been feeling a lot of anxiety and fear as a result of a traumatic event, it is advisable to consult your doctor about how best to get help from an experienced professional, so that you can try to get over the trauma in as short a period as possible.

You can find more information on Post-Traumatic Stress Disorder at these websites: http://www.ptsd.factsforhealth.org/ and

Neurobiological explanation of programming for science bods

The way that the amygdala (groups of neurons that process and memorize emotional reactions) stores these memories (or, rather, the emotional content of the memories) is that the cells and synapses (which are the little connections between brain cells) become more sensitive because of the experience the person has had and so can be "fired up" really easily. That's why a lot of therapy for post-traumatic stress focuses on cognitive behavioral therapy— in effect, reprogramming the cells. Every positive experience that you have will help to reprogram the amygdala in a positive direction (remember to start with activities you can manage without becoming too fearful), and it's that positive learning zone that exists between the comfort zone and the "way too scary" zone.

Great myths of horsemanship:
"You have to fall off 30 times to be a rider"

No, you don't! Certainly if you ride horses you need to accept that there is a chance you might fall off one day. However, to promote the idea that you *have* to fall off, that there's some benefit to it, or to tell people that it's absolutely going to happen, is totally unhelpful. Having fallen off a great many times I can't specifically recall any fall making me a "better rider" afterwards. Unless, of course, you count the times when I analyzed the fall and worked out what went wrong and so vowed not to do the same again.

For instance, if you fall off because your girth slips, then you learn always to check your girth before getting on the horse (and then again once you're mounted). I learnt early in life that you get a nasty electric shock if you stick your finger in a light bulb socket when the electricity is on. Are you willing to believe what I say, or do you feel the need to stick your finger in a socket to "make you an electrician"? If you can learn your lessons without needing proof of your mistakes, then there's no additional benefit to finding out about them practically. It's not repeating the mistake, and thereby not allowing it to happen again, that is going to improve your riding.

I know a French international jumper rider who, at the age of 26, had never fallen off. It's not a coincidence that his mother was an excellent riding instructor. And then there are all those children who have fallen off a hundred times and will more than likely give up riding by the time they reach their teens. Yes, I agree that if you *do* fall off you should get right back on as soon it is sensible to and accept that it's actually not that big a deal, but this idea that you *have* to fall off – why would you want to put that picture in your mind? Personally, I intend to sit securely and safely on every horse I ride for the rest of my life – how about you?

Experience is a dear teacher, but fools will learn from no other.

BENJAMIN FRANKLIN

http://www.rcpsych.ac.uk/mentalhealthinformation/mentalhealthproblems/posttraumaticstressdisorder/copingafteratraumaticevent.aspx

One thing that must be made absolutely clear in this early stage of the book is that if at any time you are not safe, then expressing concern and doing something about it is not being irrationally fearful or "'unconfident"; it is simply being intelligent!

Get the right instructor!

An instructor who will suit one student may not be right for another. Some students need to be asked at every step how they are feeling and whether they are ready to do more, whereas I have also seen students make tremendous improvements under the more old-school, "Come on, you can do it!"approach. It's for us as teachers to assess what is the best approach for a particular student, and then when we have lessons ourselves we need to give feedback as to what suits us better, in order to establish that a teacher is right for us.

Don't *ever* let your teacher or anyone else criticize you for having your own self-preservation at heart when you are learning to ride—listen to your fears and make the risk analysis that is appropriate for you. It may be that, for you, fear is just another word for common sense. Don't assume that professionals and top riders never feel fear; they work very hard to prepare their horses, control the conditions under which they perform and put themselves and their horses at minimum risk in any given situation. If they were riding under some of the conditions that you occasionally see at a local show, i.e. entering a jumping competition while mounted on a totally unschooled horse with no mouth and an ill-fitting saddle, they'd be frightened too, or at least have the sense to get off!

Remember, we are all influenced by the company we keep, so never be pushed into dares or tolerate bullying, however subtle.

Pat Burgess – a teacher of a lifetime

In all my time around horses I have never met a more inspirational woman than Pat Burgess. Now 76, Pat was born and brought up in Cape Town, South Africa, and was captain of the winning Western Province show-jumping team. She was the showjumping coach to the British event team from 1980 to 1989, during which time they won 5 Olympic medals and became unbeatable in the World Championships. Lucinda Green (née Prior-Palmer) won 6 Badmintons with Pat's help and still seeks her advice today. In addition to all these professional and international achievements, Pat has done an enormous amount of work with disabled riders developing the Wilton Riding for the Disabled Group as a co-organizer and instructor.

I had heard of Pat in my youth but always thought she'd be far too important to give lessons to "ordinary people," so I was star-struck when I met her at a mutual friend's lunch party. (She was most embarrassed

▽ Pat Burgess is a "living legend" who has energy, enthusiasm and the ability to inspire.

A lesson with Pat

I first met "Auntie Pat" when I was in my early twenties, and I can clearly remember this incredible lady who had the most amazing way with horses and people. She seemed to know instinctively how to get the best out of anyone; whether professional or at grass roots level.

Over the years our paths have crossed many times and she has helped me with all my horses, not least when I lost my confidence jumping. I had been working in a yard renowned for taking on horses with different problems, and I was riding a horse that was around 17hh and very narrow. We were jumping a reasonably sized fence, about 3'9" high, and parallel in the center of the arena. The horse kept shooting up to the fence and taking off, but then stopped and crashed down on top of it. My boss, who was on foot because of an injury, kept shouting at me. I wasn't worried about my safety, but I was getting upset with my boss and the situation because nothing was being achieved.

My own horses were young at the time and I didn't have to jump anything over 3' with them, so it wasn't until I went on a training course that I realized I had lost my nerve. The teacher could see what had happened so she got someone to help me repeatedly jump a small cross-rail until I felt more like my old self!

I was worried, here I was in the middle of my career and I had lost my confidence in jumping.

I was in an event barn, I loved jumping – what was I going to do? I called Pat, found out where she was teaching, borrowed back my old event horse and went to see her.

As the lesson began I remember telling Pat about what had happened and how upset I was, and I was shaking while I was talking to her.

Together we worked through some exercises and gradually I began to breathe slowly again; Pat had taught me how to replace my anxiety with concentration and had improved my thought patterns and breathing. We finished the lesson with a sensibly sized ascending spread, which the horse and I jumped spot-on with no shaking and with complete confidence! Then I remember hearing, "Oh, I forgot, we need to jump this fence off the other rein!"

So I turned and Pat changed the jump around. I cantered down to a 4'9" parallel jump, which I knew had gone up but I didn't know how high until I inspected it later! There was no anxiety, no shaking, just steady breathing – we jumped spot on. I had my confidence back.

I owe a lot to Pat and I was delighted she was in the audience when I received my British Horse Society Instructor's Certificate, as it was Pat who had helped me get there. Pat gave me the confidence to ride and compete my horses, and she has helped me understand the horses I have ridden and am yet to ride, as well as the people I have taught and am yet to teach.

SAM GOSS, IH MEMBER AND BHSI REG

when I told everyone that she was a "living legend"!) Pat is not only extremely modest but has the most enormous energy and positivity. If you want to improve your jumping, no matter what level you are at, I highly recommend going to one of her jumping clinics.

Pat also works with young people who are having a few problems, and one young man, Steve Few, believed that his time helping Pat had changed him. He said, "Pat gave me trust and respected my well-being, not caring about my past. She looked for the good in me, and even though the bad was there, Pat let me know the good was also in me and didn't stop telling me until I found it. She knew that in order to help me she had to make me help myself."

CASE STUDY

How Pat got me married!

Toby and I had been out for a lovely boozy meal with friends, and we were both lazing on the sofa talking. He was bemoaning the fact that he'd lost touch with so many of his university friends over years of job changes and moves around the country. Despite being unhappy about this, he didn't seem to consider that actually he might be able to change the situation, rather than just letting it happen. "Well," I said, "Pat always says that you must have Positive Attitude, and have the confidence that you *can* make things happen! Take control and make an effort to contact everyone you miss, and you'll be amazed at how many of them will be thrilled to hear from you. Be the catalyst, believe in yourself and make it happen." Toby lay there and considered this very thoughtfully for a few minutes.

"OK," he said, "I will make some changes to how I run my life. How's this for positive attitude—will you marry me?"

So I would like to thank Pat Burgess not only for giving me the confidence to say, "I CAN" in my riding, but also for the opportunity to say "I DO" to my husband!

ELE MILWRIGHT

PS He did contact many of his old friends, and he had the most fantastic bachelor party with 20 of them.

Some wise sayings from Pat

- First and foremost you need a positive attitude. Believe in yourself and go for it: if your mind is positive, your body is energized.
- The horse thinks in pictures—so picture in your mind exactly what you want to achieve and mentally rehearse it while with your horse so that he can pick up on it.
- Be organized, not flustered! Don't be in a rush and make sure you leave any worries behind.
- Look where you are going—not at the horse or the ground. Beam at where you want to go so your horse knows your intention.

△ With Pat you can do things you normally wouldn't dream of doing. Please note: this jump wasn't done on a whim, but after careful preparation!

Checklist

I don't want any of my readers to become a recipient of the Darwin awards, so I want to know, have you:

- completed your "thinking things through" assignment?
- done your "risk analysis" assignment?
- found the right instructor who is mindful of your safety but fills you with confidence?

CHAPTER THREE

Join the dreamers of the day

This chapter should be read on an afternoon off when you won't have any interruptions but do have plenty of time to do the assignments. Once you've done the exercises here you might like to find a time when you can get some friends over—perhaps your local Intelligent Horsemanship members or your riding club—so you can all do the assignments together. Don't be put off by the word exercises; they're not hard work, you'll find they are good fun and enlightening to do.

As the song "Happy Talk" says, when you want to achieve your dreams it's really helpful to know what they actually are. People often worry about having big dreams (or even small ones), because they feel that somehow it's "above their station" or that their friends will think they are silly and that they will only be disappointed. So, as a result they won't allow themselves to dream. Which I think is really sad.

But what if you could "dream dangerously"? What if you could achieve all that you put your mind to? What if life could be a glorious adventure of discovery, challenge and intrigue, and not simply about getting through the day and earning a living? What if it were all up to you, and you were completely free to choose the life you live? Isn't that worth exploring?

You've got to have a dream. If you don't have a dream, how you gonna make a dream come true?

"HAPPY TALK" FROM *SOUTH PACIFIC*

This is just one of a number of important assignments that you'll be expected to complete through the course of this book. So if you contact me and say, "Oh, your book didn't work for me,"(*most* unlikely, but let's just suppose) then the first question I shall be asking is, "Did you complete all your assignments?" If you didn't, then you will be sent away with a flea in your ear (whatever that means) until you have done them.

Now it's time to embark on the first assignment in the box opposite. If you can't do this assignment right now, then go and read another chapter and come back when you've got more time.

▽ *Dare to dream.*

ASSIGNMENT 1
Lottery dream

If you've ever dreamt about winning the lottery, as many people have, do you know how you would spend the money if you won? Could you write down (in as much detail as possible) exactly what you would do with the money?

I'm sure that on your list there'll be a country house with stables and indoor riding arena, and that's perfectly understandable, but I actually want a lot more detail than that. I want you to visualize clearly how your life would be if you had unlimited financial means. What are you surrounding yourself with? Who are you spending your time with? What are you doing? How does everything feel, look, smell and taste? The more senses you can engage in this daydream the better, as it helps you to clarify every last thing. You need to spend *at least* 30 minutes on this, and if you spend more time than that, even better. Please do this now, before you read any further.

ASSIGNMENT 2
The perfect day

Go get a pen and paper (or felt tips if you're a mind-mapper), because now I'd like you to plan out your perfect day. Write down every detail, using as many of your senses as you can, as described on the lottery assignment. (You've got to admit, they're nice tasks, aren't they?)

I want you to make a note of everything that will happen from the moment you wake up. Who is around when you get up (if anybody)? What is the first thing you do? What do you eat (if anything)? Do you set straight off to a big horse show to win the first class of the day?

Remember, you can do absolutely *anything* you want—I don't want you to limit yourself in any way. Perhaps you walk right out of your patio doors to stroke your horses as they graze in the field nearby? Where are you going to go in the morning? Or at lunchtime? (You can tell I think about food a lot!) What's the afternoon of your perfect day like? Perhaps your incredibly wealthy new boyfriend is taking you on a shopping trip? But where? Somewhere for coffee, or perhaps for dinner? What will you do in the evening?

See how much you can fit into one day—you might not get many days like this! Put in every detail you can think of that would make your day perfect. It's totally private to you; I'm not going to ask to see it (I promise).

When you've finished this task you might like to take a little breather. Have a cup of tea, mull over things for a while and then let's take some time to analyze what we find.

I hope you found these exercises fun to do, but be aware that they also have a very serious point to them. Many people don't actually know what they want, or they are not honest with themselves because they think they are *supposed* to want something. Therefore they believe that having aspirations makes them more acceptable to whoever is around at the time, and so they say, "I'd really like to compete at shows," or they say, "I know I'd never want to compete at a show," when really they would.

With the lottery assignment we're not interested in *what* you want, so much as *why* you want it. Look at the list you compiled during that exercise and ask a question of every detail you have written down. This house in the country, for instance, which part of that is most appealing? Is it being out of town that's important? Getting away from pollution? Being away from annoying neighbors? Or is it the feeling of space that it gives you?

Likewise with the car you've chosen—what's that going to give you? Have you chosen it because it's very safe or because it's particularly environmentally-friendly? Or is it a fast car? Or do you believe that you'll go up in people's estimation when they see you driving the latest, top-of-the-range Mercedes? What about the horses in your life? (I'm presuming there are some, but maybe not?) Start making changes immediately to bring in the essence of what you want, i.e. find alternative ways to help the environment or to build your self-esteem so that you start to feel the successes happening right away.

Again, with the perfect day assignment I want you to go back and study what you've written down—you might find it enlightening. Look at your day carefully, if you've always said that you've only ever wanted to get married and have children, and yet your perfect day has you picking up award after award for your career, this might offer you a clue as to why marriage just hasn't happened for you yet. Equally, if you say that your life's ambition is to own a boarding stable and yet on your perfect day the barn and the people you'll have to deal with are nowhere in sight, then perhaps you should think about what you find most appealing about the idea.

Perhaps you dream of being a jumper rider and yet your perfect day has you picking up the prizes at the end but not actually jumping the rounds. If this is the case then we might fairly assume that it's not that you want to do the jumping, but that you want to win the awards and the respect that this might bring you in the horse world. And this is where this exercise becomes really useful: you might discover that what you *actually* want is respect in the horse world (let's say), and once you realize this you can explore the ways in which you could achieve it that might be much more practical and enjoyable. For instance, you might train to be a showjumping judge or commentator, or you might think about owning a jumper or a share in one, or you might even go and get the qualifications and experience necessary to teach children how to jump. Keep exploring the options until you find an idea that feels right to you.

All men dream, but not all equally. Those who dream by night, in the dusty recesses of their mind, wake to find it was all vanity. But dreamers of the day are dangerous, for they may act on their dreams with open eyes and make things happen.

T.E. LAWRENCE (LAWRENCE OF ARABIA)

One more way to discover what you *really* want

When trying to get to the bottom of confidence issues it's important that we're honest with ourselves. Sometimes you discover what you want when you get that sense of, "I feel like I'm home at last," but occasionally you can make use of the darker emotions, such as that awful feeling when *envy* comes up and grips you around the stomach area. "No, no," you say, "This can't be happening to me. I'm really a *nice* person." But is envy such a deadly sin? Let's see how you might make it work *for* you, not against you.

Of course, you know that envy is a terrible thing; it is even named as one of the Seven Deadly Sins, so it really must be bad. In fact, it's so bad that it's something we don't often allow ourselves to feel; and we certainly never, ever admit to feeling it…

Having said that though, we easily spot envy in other people – especially when they're practically spitting about "how ridiculous and pretentious that woman at the barn is; swapping her two-horse trailer for a gooseneck with a tack room and dressing area. I mean, the size of it for one thing! She's only got one horse, and he's not worth two grand! She's making a complete fool of herself." Hmmm. Yes. Quite.

Then one day someone tells you about a plan they have, or they show you something they've recently acquired and you feel this incredible indignation creeping all over you. You think, "What right have they…?" Or, "Who do they think they are…?"

Envy has a negative connotation because people prefer to deny its existence, which means that these feelings then spill out as bitterness and anger, and even sabotage. However, if you acknowledge that what you're

▽ It's all very well giving advice to others – but are you following your own dreams?

really feeling is, "It's not fair, I want that horse trailer!" then honesty can put you on a far more productive path. By doing this you aren't suppressing your feelings but instead acknowledging what you really *do* want. So does that mean you're going to get it immediately? Well, no, but at least you can start planning: "So how much does a gooseneck actually cost?", "What would I need to earn to be able to buy one?", "Perhaps I could share one with someone?"

Once you've appreciated that negative feeling of envy for its only useful purpose, then it's time to let it go. If you "hate and despise" all people who are, say, self-assured and confident, who have plenty of money or own a barn of beautiful horses, then it's easy to see that your subconscious mind will always protect you from becoming one of those "terrible" people.

These emotions come, in part, from a feeling that the universe is somehow limited. If these people possess something then it might be that you believe they're taking it away from someone else—which isn't the case at all. Remember, the more each of us has, the more we can do for others. We don't say, "I'm going to be sick for the rest of my life so that other people can have good health"; that wouldn't make sense at all. And neither does worrying about not having certain things in your life. So instead, when you see people who have what you want or live the life that you aspire to, you should rejoice and say, "That's great—because if they can have and do those things, then I can have and do those things, too."

Why admitting you think someone is gorgeous can be good

When I was a jumper rider I used to see some people competing a horse who I thought was the most incredibly wonderful animal in the whole world. She was a 15.1hh chestnut mare and her name was Belmont.

Now 15-hand-chestnut mares are not everyone's cup of tea—particularly not for showjumping – but every time I was around Belmont I knew I was in the presence of greatness. She was very, very special and she could jump so quickly and accurately it was just extraordinary.

I was usually very shy, especially at that age (around 15 years old) but I couldn't resist going up to these people every time I saw them with Belmont and telling them how wonderful I thought she was and how fortunate they were to have a horse like her. I tried not to actually drool when I saw her, but you get the picture. One day, when I was 18, I got a phone call saying that Belmont's owner had been offered a job in Holland and since I loved her so much would I like to have her to compete with for 2 years?

Well if that wasn't a dream come true then I don't know what is. Of course in a perfect world I'd have been able to keep her forever, but as it was it was a privilege just to spend the time with her that I did. And I appreciated every minute of it.

Who do you have to be to achieve your dreams?

When you think about your perfect life, or even your perfect day, there's a strong possibility that the person that you are in those scenarios is not exactly the same person that you are right now. In your dream scene you might feel more content, more generous (certainly happier) and definitely more confident. But turn it on its head – which should come first? Will your perfect confidence follow on from this imagined success? Or could it be that your perfect confidence will bring about this dream of success?

What is certain is that the capacity to be confident and happy, to have a positive, optimistic outlook and to appreciate the value of the experiences

we have, is the one thing that is immediately under our control. So in the first instance, now that you have a strong picture in your mind of your personal dreams and aspirations, it is important to try to understand more about yourself.

The next three exercises are intended to help you get to grips with the person you are—both in terms of your light and your shadow.

We can discover more about ourselves by noticing the traits and behaviors in others that cause us to react negatively. Psychologist Carl Jung described this part of our personality as the "shadow"— those aspects of ourselves that we are not too proud of. Sometimes we recognize parts of our own shadow in others, and that can cause us to experience strongly negative feelings as we try to deny the shadow in ourselves.

△ *"It all depends on how you look at things, and not how they are in themselves." Carl Jung*

When my dad fell in love

I was 16 and working in the King's Stable when around 25 yearlings arrived to be broken in and prepared for the following season's two-year-old races. The lads looked through them and sorted out which they should "do"; the longest-serving lads (grooms) taking first pick.

I liked them all, but a smallish, roundish, dark-haired filly just stood out. She looked at me face-to-face—she was gorgeous. I fell in love immediately and I can never forget our first meeting. I wanted her, of course, but she went to a lad called Albert Brumby to be broken in.

Godiva, as she had been named, had the habit of flashing her tail and urinating in all directions. The breaking-in was done by the experienced lads, but she gave them a bad time —dropping them off regularly and then squirting them. They got nothing extra for the job and, knowing that I had pleaded with the head lad for a go, they persuaded him to let me try.

Godiva played with me most of the time, but she was careful not to throw me off. I hit the ground just once while cantering round our big paddock, but she stayed with me and allowed me to jump back up—not my strong suit. (The head lad said I had as much spring as a rusty penknife.)

Up until now my job at this stable had been worse than prison but now, riding my lovely filly every day, it was heaven. Then one day Brumby left and I took over as Godiva's groom as well as her rider.

In the spring of that year Godiva was working really well. She won her first race and I backed her at 6/1, but in her second race she refused to start and got herself a very bad name. A couple of jockeys were tried on her at home, but they didn't get on. It was then decided to school her under the starting gate and the head lad, Jollands, suggested, "Try her under the gate with the kid." So I rode her with Jollands and the Guvnor watching and she was no trouble.

Godiva was not the type of horse that fashionable jockeys wanted to ride. She was entered in the Stud Produce Stakes (an important event on the July course at Newmarket), but she had very little hope of winning because Gordon Richards, champion of champion jockeys, was riding the odds-on favorite, Snowberry (who had won the top Royal Ascot race for fillies—the Queen Mary Stakes). As a result, all the best fillies decided against taking her on, so it was a very small field.

On the morning of the race the Guvnor came up to me on his horse and said, "Marks, I have decided to let you ride the filly this afternoon." I couldn't take it in: a top two-year-old race against an odds-on Queen Mary winner with Gordon Richards riding? Godiva and I were just a couple of kids who had fun together.

We had no trouble going down to the start; no trouble at the gate. We jumped off at a nice, sensible pace. At the halfway stage, Gordon was cruising three or four lengths in front. He was far side, we were stands' side. It took Godiva three or four furlongs to get her act together. I waited for her to signal that she was ready and then I used hands and heels and we won by one and a half lengths. The Guvnor was pleased, but it was a very cool reception from the crowd—Gordon Richards did not get beaten at odds-on shots.

However it was different when I rode her a year later at the Oaks (the fillies' derby). During the parade Godiva gave a little buck every few yards and each time the crowd responded with "ooohs" —which encouraged her to put in an extra one that threw me off balance. But she stopped for me to right myself—she didn't want to spoil our day!

There was a lot of money for Gordon's mount, Silverlace, who was from the same stable as Drawing Prize (Silverlace was a much better racehorse than her stablemate, Drawing Prize, who Godiva and I had struggled to beat at Hurst Park) and it looked as though the extra distance might not suit us.

In the changing room I was told the jockeys were going to let me make the running again to really test Godiva's stamina. I wasn't worried; the extra work we had done and the benefit of the Hurst Park trial had got us fully fit.

We cantered quietly to the start and had our names called by our efficient gentleman starter, Captain Allison. As we lined up a couple of lengths behind the main body he said,

"Come on, Marks. Take your place." I knew the Guvnor had asked him to keep an eye on me.

My plan had been to move forward as his hand pressed the lever, but I did as I was ordered and got a fair start anyway. They went very, very fast—too fast—so that at the turn into the straight, one mile from home, we were stone last! As we came into view from the stands, "The favorite's been left!" was the cry. "Oooh" again— sadder this time. I moved to the outside, not wanting to risk going through any gaps and played a waiting game. Godiva and I were cantering while others were starting to struggle. Halfway down the straight we passed a couple of horses that the strong pace had "got to" and as we gradually closed in on the leaders at the top of the hill (where I had told the Guvnor we would make our run), Gordon Richards charged to the front to certain victory. Or so he thought.

He thought he had ridden the waiting race and saved Silverlace's energy for the finish, but Godiva had saved more. My beautiful girl ran on to win by three lengths. As we struck the front I cracked her with the whip across her quarters— and have regretted it for the rest of my life.

The racegoers gave her a tumultuous welcome and she was led in by her owner, the Hon. Esmond Harmsworth, later Lord Rothermere. He was accompanied by his lovely daughter Esme, the debutante of the year that year – but there was I, in love with a horse!

DOUGLAS MARKS

The trouble with the shadow is that the more we try to push it away, the more it tries to assert itself. Instead of ignoring or denying the darker sides of our natures, by acknowledging and understanding them we can gain a degree of mastery over them.

A very helpful exercise I use whenever I'm feeling critical or judgemental about someone is to say, "In what way am I like that?" Just the other day I was listening to someone who kept putting herself down the whole time and I was thinking, "For goodness' sake, this is so tedious. Get on with what you've got to say. We don't want to keep hearing how useless you think you are, and we know it's false modesty anyway." I was

Be the change that you want to see.

MAHATMA GHANDI

a bit surprised by my reaction because my deepest thoughts about people aren't usually that judgemental.

Thankfully this exercise—"In what way am I like that?"—comes pretty automatically to me now and I thought, "Well, I might do that a bit…" However, it did bring my reactions to my attention and I felt very embarrassed in my next horse psychology class when I realized that I had been behaving in this way for a while—a much worse trait than the one in the poor lady I was criticizing! Sure I have plenty to be humble about (there I go again!), but enough's enough.

So having this knowledge and understanding about yourself will allow you to take stock of where you are as a person, compared to where you need to be, in order to achieve your dreams. This understanding is an important basis for performing the following exercises, because once you are aware of those strengths you possess that will help you achieve what you want, and also the areas in which you need to improve, you will be able to use this knowledge to your own advantage.

How to draw your dreams towards you

In order to achieve your dreams, you need to understand that you get what you focus on.

Metaphysical aspects (our energy) has an influence on the universe and the Law of Attraction brings things and experiences that match your dominant energy patterns. On the other hand, psychologists believe that our thoughts influence our perceptions and our behaviors so that we notice and place more importance on those experiences that support our thoughts. Through consistent practice these patterns of thinking and behaving become easier and more comfortable to us, so we are encouraged to "stay put" even when things aren't working for us.

You may notice that these techniques are all focusing on the things you want to bring into your life, not the things you want to avoid. It's fair to say that, for many people, being clear about what you DON'T want can be a strong motivating factor. Perhaps your father was an alcoholic, and you're now careful with your alcohol intake because you saw what liver failure was like. Or perhaps you've never dabbled with heroin because you've seen what it's like to be a junkie and it doesn't appeal to you…

In the same way, you wouldn't want to buy a horse with sweet itch or laminitis because you've seen what distressing conditions they are.

Being clear about why you don't want certain things in your life isn't the same as obsessing on the negatives. However, it does often help to think about what you DO want, and help you to phrase it in a positive way. You want to be healthy and enjoy your life to the fullest; you'd like a horse who was happy and healthy, too. You don't just want to "not be afraid of jumping," you would also like to be confident around a course of 3' fences. When you know this about yourself you can then measure improvements on a positive scale, rather than focusing on something you're trying to diminish.

If you find it difficult to think in the positive, that's fine; that's a habit that can change. For the moment, then, just write down what you don't want and convert everything into a positive about what you do want. Don't worry at all about how to achieve any of this just now—we won't let the practicalities get in the way of our dreams! (Chapter 8 will go into the details of all that.) However, I hope that the suggestions in the following chapters can help you clarify your dreams, and work out what it is that you really want.

EXERCISE
Like attracts like

On a far more positive note, studies have been conducted into the reasons as to why people like one another and these have shown that the reason we most admire certain people is because we share important similarities with them—such as having qualities that they also possess.

Write down the names of three people whom you most admire and write down the qualities they have that you think you also have. They may not be immediately obvious but let's say that you have the capability to have those qualities: they just need polishing up a bit. That feels pretty good, doesn't it?

▽ *It's time to push out the negatives in your life...*

EXERCISE

Appreciation

Look for things to appreciate every day—that way you get more of what you focus on. These can be good or bad things; every time you focus on something you're telling the universe, "More of this, please," so keep focusing on these good things.

Every night, write down the best three things that happened that day and make it a habit to keep appreciating these things. Think of your mind as a magnet which is drawing things to you—good or bad, depending on which setting you have it on. Have you ever discovered that when a bad thing happens to you it seems like one card has been taken out of a tower of cards and everything tumbles down around you? If you've ever experienced that feeling then isn't that a good incentive for you to get back onto a positive track quickly? Don't say, "I can't think what else can go wrong now," because it's likely you'll soon find out.

Checklist

Have you:

- completed your "lottery dream" assignment?
- done your "perfect day" assignment?
- looked into any jealousy issues you have?
- decided who it is that you most admire and are drawn to?
- written out your appreciation list every evening?
- determined the qualities you need to live the life of your dreams?

CHAPTER FOUR

Old and new techniques

FOR OVERCOMING FEAR AND OPTIMIZING PERFORMANCE

Whether your current priority is to overcome a fear that's holding you back or to optimize your performance so you can achieve an elusive goal, there are plenty of useful strategies that can really help.

These strategies, and how you use them, can make the difference between feeling frustrated, inadequate and overwhelmed by life's difficulties or challenged, confident and inspired by those self-same "problems," When you see someone very successful whom you think you would like to emulate, there's a good chance that they used highly effective methods to achieve their success and if they didn't have these at their disposal they might struggle too.

Now, I wouldn't want to presume that *you* might be struggling to achieve great success in your life, but perhaps the fact that you picked up this book suggests you could do with a little help (couldn't we all?), and these next two chapters will suggest a few techniques that will help you get to wherever it is you want to be.

Don't forget, though, that knowing about these techniques is rather like people owning riding helmets—they don't work unless you use them.

What you say when you talk to yourself

Do you go out on a ride or to a competition with thoughts going round your head such as, "Oh, blast, I'm going to look like such a fool, such an idiot, such a fool, such an idiot. What will people think of me?" If this is the case then I think we need a serious talk.

◁ *"I am a very brave horse,
I am a very brave horse ..."*

My dad becomes a rider

It was the school holidays: I was 13 and weighed 60 pounds. I was restless, and it was obvious, so my father, arranged for me to go to Jim Russell, the Mablethorpe racehorse trainer, for a trial. By then I had had several riding lessons and even cantered twice, so off I went!

Every day I got up at 6 a.m., helped muck out Schweppes (the quietest, easiest ride in the stable), and then I was legged up—and away. We went on to the beach, walked and trotted for about a mile then eventually turned to canter towards home.

On our return to the paddock the lads (grooms) dismounted to let their horses graze for a few minutes. Schweppes threw me off when we reached them and wandered off. He had been so good, so why drop me now? Just when I thought I could ride. I was determined he wouldn't get away with it the next day—but he did. And the next, and the next, and the next.

Actually, he dropped me six times in the paddock. Did he think it was funny? Why was it always in the home paddock? Why not on the sea front? I had little experience of cantering and he could have easily dumped me then; but if he did, he would have to run off and behave like a horse—he could get lost, drowned, run over by a bus, become trapped in quicksand… He knew all that, and he also knew that if he did this at home he would be caught and taken in to have his meals, groomed, blanketed, and have his bed made twice a day.

He knew all that, but I have only just realized it.

So Mr. Russell called my parents and told them, "Sadly, this is not the job for your boy." They came and took me home and I didn't care if I never saw another horse.

However, my parents were very keen on racing and so it was back to the riding lessons. Mr. Kirk, the instructor, had sensible animals who helped me regain my confidence, until one day, on the sands of Cleethorpes, a dog came running towards us, barking.

"I'm going to fall off! Stop the dog!" I cried.

There was no chance of stopping the dog and Mr. Kirk's voice came over loud and clear, "You will fall off if you don't hold on. Now for heaven's sake, TRY."

Those words had the desired effect and I stayed firmly aboard my mount. And guess what? I was ready for the Grand National. Metaphorically speaking, of course.

Just that one word "try" made all the difference. Here I am at 85 years of age and I've never thought of that before. I must see if it can help my golf.

DOUGLAS MARKS

I probably don't need to point out to you that constantly repeating self-damning, negative thoughts is not good for your confidence, but I am not going to tell you *not* to think these thoughts ever again. That's practically impossible. The next time you're tempted to tell someone, "Don't worry," stop yourself and think, how can he or she "not worry"? It's like telling someone, "Don't think of pink giraffes." How can you *not* think of them until you *do* think of them? (See how you thought of pink giraffes just when I told you not to?)

In order to drive an old thought out you have to bring in a new thought, so let's replace the negative one with a positive one. This is where "affirmations" come in really handy.

Affirmations are little phrases you can memorize to say over and over to yourself in times of need (which means any time doubts creep in). The key thing with these phrases is that they are framed in terms of what you want to be or see, not the things you *don't* want to be or see.

▽ *I am on the right of the photo. I'm definitely trying and am about to win my first hurdle race.*

△ *Pie and I practicing positive affirmations and jumping.*

They need not be complicated, however. Emile Coue (the French psychologist who introduced a brilliant method of self-improvement based on optimistic autosuggestion) had as his suggested affirmation, "Every day in every way I'm getting better and better." Far better that than those free-floating, anxious thoughts whooshing around and around your brain, making you more and more fretful.

Feel free to think up your own personal affirmations. How about, "I am improving so much as a rider. Every time I focus calmly on my riding I become more competent"? Write down several and choose whichever one is most comfortable for you. The example above is useful because it incorporates the suggestion of improving while also reminding you to stay calm and focused. You could argue that this technique is a form of brainwashing (and it is), but who would you rather be brainwashed by: images on television, negative people's conversations or news agencies that profit by making people fearful or—and let's think about this carefully now – would you rather make the choice yourself?

Arguing with the "little voice"

As phobias go, mine is pretty boring. I have always been slightly envious of people who have to travel to distant jungles, dive with sharks or fly over a sunset to overcome their fears. Me, I hate heights; and not even dramatically high heights. However, for some strange reason, once I'm too high to stand a remote chance of surviving a fall, I'm fine.

One day I popped in to see a friend and we were having a giggle over her new diet hypnotherapy tape but, between sailing in a hot-air balloon over fields of food and banishing bad thoughts into boxes, there was one piece of advice that stuck with me. The therapist was talking about the "little voice" that tells you to eat and how to battle with it. I think the "little voice" comes up in all sorts of situations—for me, it was screaming, "Don't do it!" whenever I tried to climb the ladder to the top of the haystack. In fact, identifying those feelings as a voice gave me something I could argue with; something to battle against – an adversary.

Well, I am quite a determined little soul and the idea that I was being controlled by this little voice was just too much for me. It was a nice day, the horses had gone well, I had finished all the jobs early and I was on a roll. All that was left to do was the last feeds and hay nets. I needed a bale of hay. I looked up at the haystack and the voice said, "No way."

The voice and I engaged in a short battle; the voice found some other things I needed to do first, then I would come back to study the ladder again, back and forth, in jousting-tournament-style charges that came to nothing for the whole afternoon.

Eventually I plucked up the courage to ignore the voice by singing, "Oh, what a beautiful morning" so loudly that it was drowned out! But halfway up the ladder I started to feel shaky. Finally, though, I had had enough of the voice, and I decided to show it who was boss.

"I WILL CLIMB UP THIS LADDER," I said out loud rather forcefully, then I climbed up quickly before I could change my mind.

Well, I got my hay down, and I was so proud of myself, but sadly the moment didn't last. As I hoisted the hay bale onto my back, I suddenly realized I had quite an audience. I suppose my rather wobbly singing, followed by my little outburst and my scaling up the ladder faster than Spiderman had been quite entertaining. They had obviously found my battle with the voice rather less heroic from the outside than it had seemed from within. So I now get my hay down every day and I am no longer limited in any way or by any fear.

ROSIE JONES, INTELLIGENT HORSEMANSHIP RECOMMENDED ASSOCIATE

Please work particularly hard on this technique for 21 days, and after that it will become automatic and will take hardly any effort at all. By "particularly hard" I mean that the *instant* you *think* a negative thought might appear you should start repeating your affirmation.

There are immediate benefits from the first time you try this: notice how much more at ease you are and how your breathing starts to relax as you repeat your affirmations, then remain aware of how that calm place starts to become your default mode.

As we go along in this book I will teach you some more advanced techniques that will help you to create positive images in your mind. Meanwhile, I'd like to remind everyone that it's also the job of instructors, coaches, friends and parents to keep these positive pictures in the minds of those people they are supporting. I cringe when I hear parents shout at their offspring as they're going in the ring—comments like, "Now don't let him stop at that ditch!" or "Don't worry about the planks!" or "Don't think about falling off!" They are putting exactly the picture you don't want in the rider's mind!

Why can confidence be like a house of cards?

I was once asked, "Why is it that sometimes I build up my confidence and, just as I am feeling really good about myself, one little thing goes wrong and my confidence about everything else comes crashing down, a bit like a falling house of cards?"

If you've ever felt like this, please read on. There's only one common factor to all of those situations where you might lose your confidence—and that's you! The way you are feeling now has come about from how *you have explained to yourself* why something happened. When things go wrong, confident people are able to bounce back from their upset and carry on without too much trouble. They remain optimistic about their chances of future success because they have a way of thinking that says, for example, "Things go well for me because:

"I can always find a good solution to problems, whatever happens."
"This allows me to be successful in lots of different situations."
"I can handle whatever comes along."

By contrast, people who lack confidence put this way of thinking into reverse. When things go wrong they tend to see it as being their fault and usually something to do with a bad personal quality they have. For example, they might say:

"I can never make things work."
"This means I'm unsuccessful in lots of different situations."
"Things will always go wrong for me."

These people believe that they possess a bad quality that will affect other areas of their lives and will always be with them. And this is when the house of cards tumbles to the ground. The frustrating thing is that when something does go well they say, "Ah, it was just a fluke. I guess I got lucky for once in my life. But it won't last. It never does." If this sounds familiar to you, then there is good news: this is something that you can change. The key is to catch yourself doing this when you're explaining the causes of good and bad events – and then stop doing it!

△ *Here's a boy who can clearly handle whatever comes along.*

Overcoming your fears

It's impossible to know exactly how someone else is feeling, but I reckon that having lost my nerve for riding, I can relate pretty well to any of my clients who are having confidence issues.

I was about 22 and had been working for a dealer for several years, riding a variety of horses and ponies from markets and fairs. I had learnt from experience to read the horse rather than believe what I was told about his training, but a series of not-so-easy horses had dented my confidence. The final straw came while working with a big, black Russian horse.

This horse had come to us as a supposedly quiet ride who needed sedating when being shod. I worked with him until he was quiet to shoe, but the ridden work wasn't so good! I was bucked off several times, but I said "no more" when I was thrown off before I'd even got on him. At the time I had been showing him to prospective buyers—and no, they didn't buy him!

The trouble was, I made my living from riding horses, and I was in the middle of training towards my British Horse Society Assistant Instructor's certificate where I would have to jump a 3' course on a strange horse. And now I was terrified of getting on anything but the quietest horse (which wasn't much fun for anyone else, because when I get frightened I come across as very angry). So I had to decide whether to overcome this fear or change career.

However, I love horses too much, so I couldn't give up that easily! Two things helped me get over my nerves. One was the owner of the racing stable where I worked, who understood the way I was feeling. She made sure I rode the safest horses, and she gradually progressed me to the more tricky equines. The other great help was using the horses at the local riding school to help me train for my test. I explained my situation to the owner of the school, who encouraged me to have lessons on every single horse in the barn until my confidence grew.

Perhaps I will never be as brave and carefree as I was: I am certainly more careful about the horses I ride, and I spend as much time as I feel is necessary doing groundwork to establish a relationship. However, I have come to realize that caution is a good rather than a bad thing – I weigh up a situation and use appropriate skills to deal with it, rather than leaping straight in. It has also meant that I could continue my career with horses, and I now thoroughly enjoy spending time with my own horse. I also have a set of experiences and tools now that I am able to share with my clients to help them to work through similar fears.

And as I've heard many times – there's a fine line between bravery and stupidity!

SUE BROWN, INTELLIGENT HORSEMANSHIP RECOMMENDED ASSOCIATE

Understanding your adversities

Write down on a piece of paper a brief description of something bad that recently happened to you; something that you felt knocked your confidence. Try to stick solely to the facts and avoid, for the moment, giving any explanations about why this event happened.

Once you've done this, give the reasons why you think this bad event happened, including your own personal role in it.

Can you identify any points where you seem to be negatively blaming yourself for the problem? I say "negatively blaming," because you haven't yet found a way to do things better next time and effect a more successful outcome. At this stage you're feeling, "Well, that's how it is for me: it's how I am and I can't change it." So stop, and write down the reasons why you think things didn't work for you.

Flip it round

Go back to your bad situation. Can you think of any factors beyond your control that might have contributed to this situation? Was there bad weather, were there roadworks that frightened your horse or did someone else contribute to the problem somehow? (You're not allowed to give a reason and then say, "Yeah, but…" and then go on to blame yourself again.)

Now, think of a time when you did something and succeeded. It doesn't matter how small or insignificant it might seem; the size of the achievement isn't important for the moment. Write down the facts of what happened and then try to pick out as many things as you can from this positive outcome that were the result of your own personal role in it. (Again, for the purposes of this exercise, the "size" doesn't matter; all good reasons are equally important!) Keep this list to hand and, whenever you think of a new good reason, add it on. This way you will build up a handy list of all the personal reasons for your success which you can refer to whenever your confidence is wobbling.

How you can use this exercise in "real life"

To develop any new skill, you do have to practice in order to become really good. Being confident is no different. Initially you can use this exercise to begin to balance up how you explain the good and bad events in your life. When something goes wrong, instead of spending all your time focusing on the reasons why the problem was entirely your fault, try to spend just

50 percent of the time on that side and then spend the other 50 percent of the time balancing things by identifying other contributory factors that were outside your control.

In the same way, when something good happens you can acknowledge some of the "just good luck" reasons why events went well, but you could also spend even more time thinking about your own role in the success. Having taken into account all the factors that are under your control you can then practice thinking about why something will probably go well. This is the basis of confident, optimistic thinking.

The main point is that you restore some balance to your explanations, rather than just blaming yourself or bad luck, depending on which erodes your confidence the most. You don't want to swing in totally the opposite direction and go on to deny all responsibility for everything that doesn't work out; taking responsibility is good when it gives us the power to change outcomes for the future. However, it's not good if it's just used as part of, "That's just me—nothing ever works out for me." Bringing your explanations back into balance gives you the power to learn positively from your mistakes, while also acknowledging the wonderful abilities that you have.

Posture

I am grateful to my wonderful osteopath Philippa Rayne, of the Brampton Clinic, for straightening me out and explaining to me how posture affects confidence—first, in how you appear to the outside world, and so how the world responds to you. For example, "Look at hunched-up Mary over there, she's very shy, you know." But bad posture can also literally affect how we feel emotionally—it doesn't only make us *look* bad.

The involuntary nervous system, located in the ganglia by the rib-heads in the thoracic spine, can influence secretions and affect smooth-muscle contractions. For example, unconfident Mary, who is standing with her shoulders around her ears and trying to melt into the background will, with this posture, be affecting the way her guts are digesting her food; she could be feeling sick or have indigestion. Plus, her heart has less space to beat in, so she's likely to be acutely aware of her own heart beating, which will increase her feeling of anxiety. As the movement of her lungs is limited, she'll soon be feeling breathless and, before long, panicky.

▷ Pie knows when things don't go to plan: it's far more likely to be the fault of his owner than him!

Due to this unhelpful posture, the involuntary nervous system will have to work harder, which will increase activity in other areas of the spine to help these systems work properly. This will stimulate the adrenal glands, which will then make Mary anxious and completely undermine her ability to remain calm and confident. If these postures are held for a long time they are very hard to snap out of and the body will start to compensate, eventually putting strain on the joints and increasing muscle spasm and nerve irritation, leading to pain (usually in the neck or lower back). As we all know it is very difficult to appear or feel confident when we are in pain. Incorrect posture can eventually cause anxiety-pain and make you feel very depressed.

As in everything we are continually struggling for balance internally, externally, structurally and emotionally. Good posture, movement and a great osteopath are all wonderful assets to having confidence!

Breathing and distraction technique

Diaphragmatic breathing is so called because your diaphragm expands as you breathe, as opposed to shallow breathing high up in your chest (often accompanied by a squeaky voice). You feel your belly go out and your chest go in as you take a deep breath. It slows the heart rate and sends extra oxygen to your brain to take away any light-headedness and thereby allows you to apply full concentration. If you ever experience panic attacks, applying an effective breathing technique immediately is essential; but as with everything this is much better practiced when you are *not* feeling anxious, so that it becomes easy to apply when you do feel stressed.

An easy way to achieve this breathing is to place one finger across under your nose. Try it, and breathe in. Isn't that clever? Remember this for stressful times and don't worry if people think you're strange! Concentrating on breathing can also act as a good distraction technique when teaching nervous riders. I ask my students to breathe in to the four footfalls of the horse's walk, and then breathe out to the next four. Just asking a student to count the footfalls helps her to tune into the horse, while she starts to forget about her nerves by concentrating on the footfalls. I will also ask her to walk the horse over a pole, naming which foot she is using to step over the pole without looking down. In my lessons with Pat Burgess (see page 50) I found that I was often concentrating so hard on keeping a good lower leg position, I didn't notice that the jumps were getting higher and higher. A good teacher needs equal amounts of sympathy and motivation, with a little cunning thrown in!

Hypnotizing yourself

Self-hypnosis is a naturally occurring state of mind that can be defined as a heightened state of focused concentration (a trance) with the willingness to follow instructions (suggestibility).

It is not a magical state; it is merely a state of mind in which:

You are very relaxed.

You are paying complete attention to the suggestions you want to implant.

You do not criticize the suggestions made, but accept them at face value.

▽ To help you to relax, imagine beautiful scenery and calm images.

Because you are in this relaxed state the affirmations and suggestions you make can travel directly to your subconscious mind, while at the same time reducing your stress level and inducing relaxation.

The first few times that you use self-hypnosis, find a place where you can remain undisturbed for a while. Sit or lie down, eliminate any distractions and relax. This puts you in the best possible conditions for using the technique – however, as you get more practice you will find that you can use self-hypnosis almost anywhere that it is safe to do so. Obviously, don't try this while you're driving a car, riding a horse or doing something else that requires your full attention!

So, the first step is to relax: close your eyes and, using images of waves of relaxation running down your body from your scalp downwards, try to wash out your stress. Let the waves run in time with your breathing: first, washing down over your head, then your neck, then your torso, then your arms and finally your legs. Feel the muscles in your body soften as the waves of relaxation wash over them.

Alternative techniques can involve fixing your eyes on a spot on the wall or imagining yourself riding down in an elevator from the top of a tall building, slowly dropping down into relaxation and drowsiness. The method you choose to use to induce your own hypnosis is up to you.

The next step is to use suggestion to deepen the state of hypnosis. This is as simple as saying to yourself something like, "I am feeling comfortable and relaxed. With every breath I am becoming more comfortable and relaxed." You can then add an affirmation of your choice, such as, "Every day I notice how confidently I handle every situation that arises."

If you find it difficult at first to get into a relaxed state, you may find it helpful to use a hypnosis or guided visualization CD. It's a good idea to buy one from a large record store where you can listen to it first—it's not much help if you find the speaker's voice irritating! (Some of these CDs even advertise "Female, American narrator"!) At the very least, spending some time regularly—preferably every day—relaxing in this way can be very beneficial to your general physical and emotional well-being.

Once you're experienced at using this technique you might even want to make your own CD of suggestions, or simply add new affirmations over a period of time, as your "old" ones become engrained. Practiced regularly, this technique can do wonders for both your confidence and your performance, but it can also help you with any other goals you might want to achieve, such as losing weight, stopping smoking an "installing" desirable habits.

Celebrate every success

Don't wait until you've won the Olympics to celebrate your successes; try to find something to appreciate in your horse and yourself every day.

Sadly, many of us remember our bad times and failures more than we do our successes. There are some people who, if they have a good horse or great people around them, just take it for granted. They ignore all the good things that people do and only communicate with them to tell them off if they get anything wrong. Would you want to be around a person like that?

▽ *Let waves of relaxation wash over you.*

Celebrating success with Thor

Sometimes we can be too hard on ourselves and only concentrate on what we would like to achieve, instead of what we have actually achieved. This was brought home to me recently as I thought about Thor, who had been on stall rest for four weeks with severe ligament damage.

I found myself sitting down with him and giving him a nice old cuddle while he lay down on his newly laid bed. What was remarkable about this situation was that a year earlier he wouldn't even have gone into a stable. He was absolutely terrified of them—having never been into one—and I spent two or three weeks just getting him to stay inside long enough to eat his supper. Patience paid off, however, and thank goodness it did.

Similarly, I started him on the horse walker for 5 minutes, and I had to admit that I didn't know what to expect. He moved calmly to the walker, went straight in and, although he bucked on his way round, he basically behaved very well. As I opened the gate to collect him, he was towering over me and doing a very good impression of a snorting, stomping stallion. I asked him to move back out of my space, which he did immediately, and I started to lead him out. He was extremely excited, and had discovered a new-found interest in everything from stones to wheelbarrows (thank the Lord for the invention of the Dually halter). However, every time he became overenthusiastic I said, "Wait," and that's just what he did. He also went straight back into his stall without any fuss at all.

Now this might not sound like much of an achievement, but when I first bought him he walked all over me, even when he was out at grass all summer. To be in a situation where I could bring this huge fella out of his stall after four weeks of confinement and still be able to control the proceedings was quite amazing. It made me think, though: it's very easy for us to pat ourselves on the back when we've just won the top prize in a dressage competition or jumped our first clear round, but do we ever congratulate ourselves on a daily basis? The irony is that it's these smaller (seemingly insignificant) achievements that allow us to win the prizes or have the larger successes in the long term. It's not just about how you perform on the day; it's about all the hard work that you put in without necessarily realizing you're doing it.

So next time you're in the arena and your horse knocks a pole, don't be disheartened—at least he tried to jump it! If he steps around the outside of the puddle, well, look on the bright side—this time he was nearly brave enough to get his feet wet.

LISA CULLIMORE

▷ *Make the most of your successes: Pie and Daisy winning BSPS Rider of the Year for the second time.*

But suppose you are that person, and you're also the person that you are treating badly. Well, that would be crazy, wouldn't it? It's just a bad habit, though, and a habit you can change. Practice looking for all the things you and your horse are getting right—and praise yourself!

Keep a success journal

Make a point of writing down your successes every day—whether they are big or small. "Even though I was tired, I managed to cook a quick and healthy meal." That's worth celebrating: after all, lots of people live on macaroni and cheese and takeout. Also include acts of kindness, refraining from sarcastic comments and keeping your commitments and focus on the positive. Even if you struggled with your canter transitions, if you got one good one then mention it. If you didn't get even one, but you've worked out what was going wrong, jot that down. If you couldn't work out what was going wrong, but you managed to stay cool, then make a note of it.

If you had a serious sense-of-humor breakdown, this is the time to regain perspective. "I had a highly productive riding session in which I learned at least five different ways how not to get a canter—I think I might even have invented one." Remember, Thomas Edison, the inventor of the light bulb, even tried peanut butter in his desperation to find a conductor for his bulb filaments. "I have found 10,000 ways that don't work," he said optimistically, and it was these that led him eventually to discover what *did* work. If he hadn't persisted, we might still be reliant on candles.

As a separate exercise, write down your lifetime's achievements: anything you've done that you makes you feel good about yourself. You don't have to have won the championship at your County Show; maybe it was reassuring your horse in the right way when he was frightened, or maybe it was standing up to the barn bully or helping a stranger at a show. I'm picking horsey examples, but I actually want to you to pick each and every example you can think of and write it down. The idea is to find things that you can celebrate about yourself. It's time you recognized all those strengths you have, but haven't been acknowledging.

Set up a good support system

Find a success buddy. It doesn't matter if you're dieting, writing a book or planning to compete your horse; having someone to support you, compare notes with and see you through the dark days can make all the difference.

Make sure you both understand that your purpose is to grow and improve. Keep your goals in mind and remind each other how far you've come.

On the other hand, you should be aware that sometimes when you start to put these new ways of thinking and behaving into action, you can end up meeting quite some resistance from the people around you – even the ones who love you! Expect the best of your friends and family, but at the same time, be prepared for the possibility that some people might not be as enthusiastic about the changes you are making as you are. Sometimes it's wise to keep things to yourself when speaking to certain people, especially if you think telling them something will make them feel insecure.

You're not required by law to tell everyone everything that you are thinking and doing and why. Put these new techniques into place and let those around you notice for themselves how much more confident and positive you're becoming. When they ask how you did it, you will be able to recount your own experience as proof that these techniques work.

▽ *You always feel better if you have a good support system around you.*

I get by with a little help from my friends

One of the things I love about Intelligent Horsemanship is the amount of support we can obtain from each other. We're all riding on the same tide— and it's so much more fun that way. Winning the Ladies European Championship in Vienna was made even more wonderful by the fact that I was lucky enough to form a really good friendship with the Swedish rider, Pia Alquist. She was so lovely and she said that if she wasn't meant to win it she was just so glad it was me – and she was totally genuine.

It was as I was on the plane home, though, that I felt a touch lonely. I was sitting on my own and saw the British Swimming Team were on the same flight, celebrating their European silver medal win. I thought, how lucky they were to have each other to share the experience. When I arrived home I experienced that weird feeling you get when you've completed a "life's goal" —it leaves you thinking, "So what do I do with the rest of my life?" Answer: "Start making other goals quickly!" I realized that whatever I did in the future, I wanted to be part of a team. My Lone Ranger days were over!

You are five minutes away from being confident

I told you this book really works. I bet that when you started you imagined that it was going to take you a while to reach the point where you could say you were a confident person capable of achieving your dreams. Well, there's good news and there's bad news. The bad news is that to achieve your dreams you're going to have to work on this every single day; the good news is that every day that you work on them, you are achieving them. You see, these techniques and tips will discourage you from going back to doing and thinking in the old, tired ways. Every 5 minutes that you spend on this, you are on your way to achieving your goals.

Abraham Maslow wrote about the Hierarchy of Needs Pyramid, which represented what he believed each of us need to live a fulfilled life (http://en.wikipedia.org/wiki/Maslow's_hierarchy_of_needs). Maslow put "self-actualization" (the technical word for achieving your dreams) at the top of the pyramid and described how this was "a state where the journey becomes the goal, not the destination." The most important thing for you to do now is to start making this a program that you incorporate into your everyday life—even if it's just a question of making those changes for 5 minutes at a time and building up from there.

Take it slowly

First, making this a program doesn't have to mean adding in everything all at once. If we wanted our horse to learn something new, a totally new way of behaving, we wouldn't simply expect him to change overnight. We would take things step by step and bring in new things that we thought he could cope with, one at a time. But we would also make sure that he was progressing as quickly as he could.

In the same way, you need to take these techniques one step at a time: it's OK to start with the ones you think you will find the easiest to incorporate into your program. In fact, starting with the easiest steps is a good way to begin because it will help you build your confidence and motivation.

▽ *The journey, rather than the destination, becomes the goal.*

Check your progress

You should ensure that you *are* always making progress, though. Once you're familiar with a technique and have been using it every day, you should tackle the next-easiest technique—and so on. What you're looking to do is to incorporate these new methods gradually until they become a series of good habits for you. So start with the technique you feel most drawn to; the one that you feel you could attempt and practice until it becomes familiar and more of a habit. You can even practice using these techniques in other parts of your life, such as your work or family life, not necessarily only in those parts associated with horses and riding.

As an example, one of the ways I made a habit of using affirmations was to write them on a piece of paper and then stick them everywhere around the house; seeing them would remind me to repeat the affirmations to myself regularly. It's a good idea to stick a note with an affirmation next to the bathroom or bedroom mirror and say it to your reflection when you have a quick check on how you're looking during the day! That way, you not only say your affirmation, you also replace the almost inevitable self-critical remark such as, "My hair looks so bad!" with something much more positive.

I stick positive messages on my computer and use my screensaver for the same purpose, too. You could include affirmations into your horsemanship by sticking the note on your car dashboard for your drive to the barn, or even next to your tack or grooming equipment. The main thing is to put reminders where you will come across them; in the early days especially you will need to find ways in which you can support yourself as you try to incorporate these new attitudes in your everyday life.

Stay motivated

In any process of change there's a period of time when you will feel as though it's hard work establishing the new changes. However, if you try to make change as fun and easy to incorporate as possible, it will help you to stay focused and motivated. Use your "perfect day" assignment (see page 58) as a way of reminding yourself of the wonderful rewards that are out there for you, and remember to keep in touch with your success buddy. You could even monitor each other, checking you're both keeping to "the rules," or hold little competitions with each other on the various assignments. Be prepared, though, that it might feel a bit of a struggle from time to time (that's what makes us grow!). Sometimes it *is* going to require willpower and effort, but that's all right—you can do it!

Checklist

- Are you saying positive things when you talk to yourself?
- Are you making sure that your "little voice" is on your side?
- Have you completed your "understanding your adversities" assignment?
- How are you working on your posture? Pilates? Yoga? Alexander Technique?
- Are you doing your diaphragmatic breathing?
- Are you performing your self-hypnosis techniques?
- Have you been celebrating your successes? (Think of an example of success now.)
- Are you keeping your success journal?
- Have you written out your achievements?
- What ways have you thought of to stay motivated?

CHAPTER FIVE

Mind games that work

"The Science of Success" — aka NLP (Neuro Linguistic Programming)

I started studying Neuro Linguistic Programming in the 1980s when people thought you were *really* weird (not just averagely so) when you tried to explain what it was. There are some extremely useful ideas in NLP, and I like the way it concentrates on positive possibilities and how the mind works to produce results.

Traditional clinical psychology tends to focus on analyzing problems and their causes. This can be very useful in understanding certain aspects of your behavior, but not if the conclusions you draw are along the lines of, "Well, of course I'll never succeed—look at my childhood!" I'm not being unsympathetic about traumatic experiences, it's just that you need to recognize that whatever happened in the past, you now have the choice to go on and make the changes you want for your life in the future.

NLP has also been the subject of some wilder claims and has a rich and varied past; it is this reputation that has caused its cofounder, John Grinder, to have reservations about what it's become in the hands of the many people who have adopted it as their own. If you're interested in hearing the full story of the mayhem, mystery and murder (literally) that accompanies NLP, the free online encyclopedia, Wikipedia, has some interesting reading on the subject (http://en.wikipedia.org/wiki/Neuro-linguistic_programming).

◁ *Always try to look for solutions, not problems.*

Being an Olympic gymnast in a Swish

Here I'm going to suggest using a version of Richard Bandler's "Swish technique," whereby you learn to automatically swap one (negative) thought for a new (positive) thought. There are variations of this technique written up in a few books, but if you want to get the full details straight from the source then read Bandler's book, *Using Your Brain for a Change*.

This technique is excellent if you have an unpleasant memory or an unpleasant or demotivating thought that you want to replace with a positive or motivating thought. For example: I'll go back to the last time Pie bucked me off. What actually happened was: I lay on the ground for a while trying to get my breath back, I was a bit sore when I managed to stand up and I ached for a while afterwards. Now I'm going to change that image.

So, I'll imagine it all as if I'm watching it happen to someone else. This is called "disassociation"; you will have experienced this if you've ever been in an accident and everything went into slow motion, or even if you've been a spectator to such an event. This is nature's way of protecting you from experiencing anything more than your mind can cope with. So, as I'm watching the picture I'm making it very small and in black and white and watching it go further and further away. It's so pale now that the picture's translucent and as it's totally out of sight—"Swish!"—we're ready to put a new story is in its place. Now, instead of watching the event I found myself experiencing, I see a completely different scenario. Now, instead of seeing the event as I did before, I am now watching a completely different film. This time as I land on the ground I roll over several times. I'm laughing. I can feel the energy in my body. This whole picture is big and in full color with inspirational music and people clapping and cheering. I leap up off the ground like a gymnast, saying, "Ta-da," and the people all around are laughing and applauding me. Now, for good measure, I think I'll vault back on him.

OK, so now it's your turn. Think of an experience you've had that isn't doing you any favors. Watch it as if it's happening to somebody else. Put the picture in black and white. Let it go further and further away from you, until it's so pale that it's nearly translucent. It's going further and further away. Then—"Swish!"—put in your new experience. *Feel* how funny it was; how strong and capable you are. See the people's faces as they admire your agility. Hear people talking admiringly about you. Isn't it great?

The conscious mind is the office boy;
the subconscious is the CEO.

RICHARD BANDLER

You can go through this over and over again until every time you try to think of the "bad" picture you're automatically taken straight to the "good" one. Make sure that each time you do the exercise after the good story you "break your state," which means getting out of the previous state of mind and thinking of something else entirely. This prevents you from automatically coming out of the negative state straight into the positive,

▽ *Keep your mind on the ups – not the downs.*

but then only to go right back into the negative. So, in order to do this you could think of something else entirely, such as the annoying, "If a tree falls in a forest and there's no one to hear it, does it make a sound?" Or you could listen to the radio for a while until you forget what you were thinking about before.

Ideally, you would get a practiced professional to work through this exercise with you. If you're going to pay a professional, though, make sure he or she is worth the money and has some record of success. You could ask a friend to work through the exercises with you if you can't afford to pay a professional. Either way, don't be naughty and skip this exercise indefinitely, then claim the book didn't help you; if you really give this exercise your maximum effort I can guarantee that the next time you think of the "incident" your happy association will immediately pop into your head.

"But," you might respond, "I had a fall once and I didn't enjoy it at all. That's the reality, and I don't see how swishing in a fake memory is going to help!" Well, it's important to understand that, however vivid, the memories in themselves aren't actually *real*. The memory is just a representation of an event that happened—a mental reconstruction of that event. So you might as well reconstruct it in a way that's positive.

The fact is, I did have that fall off Pie. Once. But if I don't swish the memory, then every time I remember it it's as if I've had the fall again. As studies into memory and perception have shown, during both the storage and retrieval of memories in the brain, there is often little difference between visual images created by the senses (i.e. those you experienced in reality) and those created by your imagination. Would you go out every day and physically practice doing something badly? Do you get on your horse, think things through and say, "Today I'll practice riding really badly. I'll make sure I'm unbalanced and tip from side to side and will keep catching my horse in the mouth until he can't stand it any longer. I'll aim to fall off at least ten times."

I'm guessing you don't do that. So can you see the harm you are doing yourself by practicing this in your head? That's why I want you to stop it. Right now! As Andrew Hoy described in an earlier chapter, before he jumps a cross-country course at an event, he visualizes jumping the obstacles *successfully* at least three times before he attempts the course. This is a technique that is used throughout the sports world by professional competitors.

ASSIGNMENT
Get the music in you!

Another NLP term is "Anchoring"—a real goody, and more deliberate than just a pleasant, confidence-giving association. Anchoring is an external event, say, a piece of music, or a word ("Yes!"), or a symbol you see in your mind, or a physical feeling (such as your thumb clenched against the middle finger), which triggers an internal state or brings up a positive memory. For example, if you get a warm glow and recall happy memories when you hear a particular piece of music, then the *music* is functioning as an anchor. Smells can also be extremely powerful in taking you to a certain place and frame of mind.

Anchors may be accidental—you feel happy to hear that piece of music because it was playing all the time during your wonderful summer romance (or maybe you hate it now for the very same reason!), but it's good to make anchors deliberately so you can get yourself into a resourceful state at a moment's notice. I've found that one of the best ways to do this is to use the thumb–middle finger anchor, along with a silent "Yes!" when anything great happens. I can discreetly use this any time I want to access that great feeling, and it will instantly take me back to a special time when I felt on top form.

I'd like you to go out today and get yourself a theme song. Monty Roberts' theme song for his demonstrations is "In a Big Country." It's a tune that's very moving and emotional anyway, but whenever I hear it my heart starts beating faster because I start to think I've got 20 seconds before I go out and introduce Monty! I have my own theme music, which comes from *Dances with Wolves*, which I use for my own demonstrations. When I hear that tune I go all tingly and forget everything else except going in to the arena to show people good ways to work with horses—terrific!

Here are a few inspirational songs you could try—you could even use them as your ringtone!

"Survivor" – Destiny's Child

Competition folks may go for a horse show theme, such as the
finale from Mozart's "Musical Joke"

Olympic hopefuls may be drawn to "Chariots of Fire"

My horse Pie's favorite is "Simply the Best"

"I Will Survive" – Gloria Gaynor

"That Don't Impress Me Much" – Shania Twain
(good when you're around big-headed people)

If you think that any of these pump up too much adrenalin in you (even if it's in a positive way), then you might like to pick something a little gentler to calm you and your horse.

Listen to your theme tune. Feel the confidence well up in you. Could you play that music next time you are riding in a schooling arena? Work out a way you could incorporate the music into your training one day, or at least play it in your car on the way to the stables.

The other reason why this method of playing or singing positive songs is effective is because it quietens those free-floating, anxious thoughts that often dominate our conscious mind, and immediately replaces them with positive lyrics – just like a musical version of using affirmations. Singing also helps to regulate your breathing and helps you to breathe more deeply and regularly, which in turn helps to regulate your heartbeat in anxious situations. So, for many reasons, this exercise is highly effective at helping you develop and maintain your confidence when you need it most.

More techniques for the nervous

I asked my nervous client to get on her horse in the style of different people – she did Marilyn Monroe, Elton John, her mother! In the end she mounted over 12 times and really got over her fear of getting up there – she hadn't been on him in over a year.

When on him, she said, "I don't deserve this; I'm not a good enough rider. Something will go wrong." Rather than argue about these points, I had her repeat the same lines in a silly voice. She laughed and relaxed, and then later in the session she suddenly started giggling. She explained that she'd started to think those things again and heard the silly voice, which made her laugh. It worked really well.

ROSIE JONES, INTELLIGENT HORSEMANSHIP RECOMMENDED ASSOCIATE

Dressage to music (in a fashion)

"Enter at working trot, X halt, salute, proceed at working trot."

My brother's horse, Mandy, would invariably rear when he asked her to halt at the beginning of a dressage test. This didn't happen when I was riding her or when he was training at home, and eventually we surmised that it was because he was nervous and tense, and this was her way of reacting, being a sensitive mare.

I don't remember where we picked up the tip, but he learned to sing nursery rhymes to himself as he rode down the center line (preferably not "Humpty Dumpty had a big fall"!) and the problem was solved. Many times since I've used this trick, both with adults and children, to encourage relaxation and fun. Personally I believe that, along with taking your mind off the scary issue, the laughter (few people can fail to laugh at themselves singing a nursery rhyme out loud) encourages engagement of the core stability muscles, which sends a strong signal to your horse (at least from your body, if not from your mind) that you are in control.

SUE BROWN, INTELLIGENT HORSEMANSHIP RECOMMENDED ASSOCIATE

Incidentally, if I'm ever nervous or have doubts about going to work in front of an audience, I imagine the following: that there's one person in the audience who really needs the help and information I can give. I don't think about anyone else in the audience but just the things I can say to that one person. Have you ever been to one of my demonstrations? Because, if you have, did you realize it was *you* I was talking to that night?

Visualization or "mental rehearsal"

All the top athletes use this technique in competition, but that doesn't mean you can't use it before you go out on a hack. Ask yourself, what is it you want to achieve? Put your imagination to work for you and do a mental rehearsal of yourself performing perfectly whatever it is you need to do.

The term "visualization" is one that you will have heard a lot, but it can be misleading, so I prefer the term "mental rehearsal." It's not about watching yourself as if you're on TV (as with disassociation); you need to see, feel, touch, taste and smell the experience through your own senses —as if it's actually happening to you in the here and now.

I remember a time when I used mental rehearsal extensively before a race. I was riding a lovely mare called Crackling in the richest Ladies' Handicap race of the year at Newbury: a Group One racecourse. (In a Handicap Race the horses that have won a lot that season carry higher weights.) There was over $20,000 to the winner, and my dad and the three other guys who owned Crackling all needed the money!

Crackling was just a little thing, maybe 14.3hh, and she hadn't won a race for nearly two years. But that wasn't all bad news, because it meant she had a low weight to carry (but it was bad news for me as I would have to diet!) and she was a good price—meaning my dad and the other owners could win a decent amount through betting if she won. As a Lady Amateur Jockey I didn't get to ride in *that* many races a year, and Crackling being a little sweetie and Newbury being my local racecourse, well, I just thought it would be a real dream to win there…

So I really, really wanted to win this race; to help me achieve this, I put my mental rehearsal together with my fitness plan. There's a long hill going up to a farm in Upper Lambourn, Berkshire, so every evening I would ride my bike up that hill without sitting down on the saddle. (Doing this really works your thighs, which can get tired when you're urging your horse on at the end of a race.) I'd ride up to the top of the hill, and my legs would be killing me, but I would see this big stone outside the farm and I made that my imaginary winning post. I'd push so hard on the pedals and imagine the bike was Crackling in the race, and as I came up to the stone I'd say, "Come on, Crackling!"

Every time, I won. Even my dog Willoughby played the game—and he always let me beat him by at least a short head. Then I'd freewheel my bike down the hill and I'd ride back up to win again. I did that nearly every day for a month: sometimes it was close, but we always, always won.

When you've won a race that often it's quite weird when you're in the weighing room getting changed for it. I remember not being chatty in the changing room beforehand and one of the girls joked that when I was like that I had something up my sleeve. I recollect going out to get mounted on to Crackling in the paddock, where the owners were making jokes as a way of dealing with their nerves; but I didn't really hear them or understand the jokes, I just wanted to get on and get to the start. It was a long canter down, 6 furlongs, and Crackling was really strong; I had to keep her head at an angle so she couldn't get any speed up and waste energy, but I also talked to her to relax her.

The race was set over a mile and a half and there were 21 runners. I was drawn on the wide outside of all the other runners as number 21. My dad had told me to keep to the inside, as we couldn't afford to give a yard away if she was to have any chance of winning. From the position I was drawn, that advice was impossible to follow, but I noted it without worrying. When the gates opened we were slow jumping out (I forgot to mentally rehearse that!), but I didn't concern myself as there was a long way to the finish line and the others had gone off very, very fast. (I heard later that the owners, watching from the stands, all groaned when they saw we jumped out last.) With everyone way in front of me now I let her gradually drift over to the inside. After 7 furlongs we were approaching the bend round the home turn, and then we were on the inside rail—but with 21 horses to get past.

Well, you've got to know that sometimes miracles do happen, because what happened that afternoon was, for me, the equivalent of Moses parting the Red Sea. Every single horse in the race went wide on the bend. Every single horse except little Crackling, of course, who (I'll swear she breathed in) sneaked her way up on the inside, overtaking one horse, then another horse, then another. And with a furlong to go there were just three more to overtake—including the favorite.

I saw the rider of the favorite bring her whip up and start whipping her horse furiously, and I thought, "Come on, Crackling"—though I have to say it was harder pushing in this race than it was riding my bike and I could feel my legs starting to weaken. So I just kept my mind on the stone —I mean the winning post—and pushed and pushed and kept her straight.

The winning feeling was completely amazing, because for a minute I couldn't tell the difference between reality and fantasy. Was I suddenly going to find that Cracking was really just an old bike, and the winning post a stone, and then look at the crowds of Newbury only to find I was just looking over the fields of Maddle Farm? The BBC commentator reported on the replay, "What an amazing race. Kelly Marks resisted the temptation to go for her whip and won with hands and heels!"

"Resisted the temptation"? I don't think so. That was never in the plan. This one was always going to be won by Crackling and me in partnership.

▷ *Crackling winning at Newbury; but I'd won this race 100 times before – but only in my mind.*

A story about me "modeling" in my teens (Twiggy and me)

Another very useful NLP approach is "modeling"; if we can exactly replicate or model the thinking and behavior of people who are successful, in whatever they are doing, down to the smallest of details (even the way they breathe, move and think), then we too can achieve similar results.

When I was in my teens I had an experience that really helped my shyness. I knew I was very shy because I felt extremely awkward around people I didn't know and I dreaded the walking into a roomful of unfamiliar faces or—God forbid—starting up any sort of conversation with someone new. I think many people feel a bit like this but, as with everything else, if you develop a workable strategy it doesn't have to be a problem.

One day I went to the house of my friends Richard and Michael Hills, and they had a friend with them who had received a lot of publicity before he'd even arrived. Steve Cauthen was known as the "Six Million Dollar Kid" at the time, as he was a jockey who had won that sum in prize money in America although he was still only 19 years old. I think meeting somebody "famous" is even more daunting for most of us than meeting someone "normal." I immediately wondered if I could just walk back out of the door without anyone noticing, or maybe if I willed it enough I could just vaporize and nobody would be any the wiser that I'd been there.

However, before I had time to act out either of those scenarios, Steve did something I remember clearly to this day—he looked me in the eye, smiled and seemed delighted to see me, then he stretched out his hand as he walked over, saying, "Hi, I'm Steve Cauthen—pleased to meet you." Now, aside from being totally charmed by these gorgeous American manners, a life-changing thought went instantly through my head: "I could do that!" I could look people in the eye, smile, look pleased to see them, shake their hand and say, "Hello, I'm Kelly Marks. How do you do?" (The English version!)

After a while I realized that I might not actually be shy, but because I hadn't found any confident role models to copy *I simply didn't know what I was meant to do when I met people.* I suggest you stop thinking of confidence as something you *are*, and instead realize that it's actually something you can *do*.

◁ *Today, I'm going to be... Zara Phillips!*

Find a role model

So, as the psychiatrists say, "We're not here to talk about me"; let's take some time to talk about your situation. Who are *your* role models for different situations? Could you list them, please? You may have confident people around you, but if you don't respect and admire them and if, for instance, you think all confident people are "big-headed and insensitive," you won't want to be like them—and that will be taking you even further from your goals.

You've got to find someone you respect and admire who has the qualities that you aspire to, and you need to spend time around them and copy them. (Discreetly, of course, you don't want to become a stalker!) If you can't physically spend time with them, you could still imitate them by watching them on video. This is extremely good if there's a rider you particularly admire who has produced a training video. Why not watch it whenever you've got 10 minutes in front of the TV? If there's any part you don't like, don't watch it. Just watch the behavior that you would like to emulate.

Watching highly competent performances can help you draw in skills as if by osmosis: ever noticed how your tennis improves after the US Open (if you watched it on television!)? Similarly, who has the kind of relationship with horses that you'd like right now? Get to know them. Study the qualities that they possess that you would really like. If possible, read their autobiography, ask them the questions you'd really like to know, take lessons, take them out to lunch, marry them – do whatever it takes!

Acting the part

If you act the part long enough you can actually *become* the part. Acting "as if" works in myriad different ways. As with all things, we need to check that it's working *for* us, rather than against us. I heard some friends the other day discussing a neighbor who plays the dumb blond with increasingly more conviction. "I mean, Shelley couldn't really be that dumb," said one of them. But on weighing up the evidence, she decided that Shelley had been playing the part so long, she'd actually become the part!

I wouldn't advise playing such an unproductive role, but I can't think of any reason why you can't be a "top performer" if you put your mind to it. I remember one of my very first students doing her first Join Up—one of the forms of bonding work we do with the different horses on our courses. She had been to Monty's demonstrations several times, and goodness knows how many times she had watched his videos. The first time she went in to do a Join Up with a horse, it was so well done that it was extraordinary, and I told her so. The only thing I found a little curious was the way she picked up the saddle; as if she was in a lot of pain. I said to her, "What made you pick up the saddle that way?" She went back in her mind and replied, "I guess because that's the way Monty does it." She wasn't just imitating Monty; she had *become* Monty. She had modeled him completely—right down to the last detail. There was no problem with the way she picked up the saddle, but I did explain to her, "Monty picks up the saddle like that because he has pain from back surgery—there's really no need for you to do it like that, unless you want to!"

▽ *Me on the far right "acting the part" of a jockey and beating the Champion Male Amateur of the Year.*

Delusion alert!

"Isn't there just a whiff of risk, though," you ask, "that we start to delude ourselves into thinking, not only that we're someone that we're not, but that we're in fact better than we really are?" This is most unlikely: those prone to delusion would be most unlikely to pick up a book like this. Why would such people even consider changing themselves in any way?

For the rest of us who do constantly ask whether we're on the right track then question that we're questioning it ("I shouldn't be questioning all the time, if I were more confident I wouldn't question…"), you'll find a comment from Dr. Raj Persaud's book *The Motivated Mind* reassuring. He notes that, "The most motivated and successful people harbor fears that their belief in their current strategy might be mistaken—hence their tendency to question their approach and be open-minded to other ideas. The less motivated, and those who suffer from false hope syndrome, tend to not fear enough being wrong and so overly believe their current approach is right. As a result they are more prone to not achieving their goals."

I think it's fair to say that the delusional and overconfident, together with the thoroughly insensitive (funny how those things often go together), are out there – and thanks to the good doctor we can now make a case for superiority among us who are still questioning our abilities!

If you can't find a great role model, here are some tips on what confident people *don't* do

- They don't resist new experiences that may be exciting or beneficial.
- They have a relaxed attitude towards life.
- Their movements are fairly smooth; they don't appear to be rushing around, out of control.
- They don't apologize constantly or say things to put themselves down, such as, "Well, that's just me. I'm such an idiot." Scientific studies have actually shown that saying negative things to ourselves like this actively weakens our muscle strength at the time we say them, and it can even lower our immune system. So this one really has to stop!

The whole problem with the world is that fools and fanatics are always so certain of themselves, but wiser people so full of doubts.

BERTRAND RUSSELL

However, if you are concerned that you are in some fool's paradise about how well things seem to be going, you may just like to work through a quick reality check:

1. Do friends and colleagues tend to look bemused when you tell them your plans and what you've been up to?
2. Have two or more close friends told you the same thing but you refuse to listen, and in fact you just avoid them now?

3. Does your experience of events seem to be very different to others who were around at the same time?
4. Do you find yourself practicing stories and excuses way ahead of conversations so that after a while you convince *yourself* the exaggerations (or even downright lies) are actually true?
5. Do you talk about yourself all the time but it never occurs to you that other people might have anything worthwhile to say?

Results:

Mostly "No" answers:

It doesn't look like you have a problem with reality.

Mostly "Yes" answers:

Let's face it, it doesn't really matter what I write here because you're just reading, "Others put you down because they're jealous of your success, they don't understand you because you're the best, you're just wonderful, you're the greatest, you're the funniest, you're the wittiest…"

Checklist

Please look through the checklist and make sure you have completed all your assignments. It might feel like it uses up a lot of brainpower but it really will be worth it, because after that you're ready to progress to the next chapter, which is *really* good. This is where you are going to learn to be your own best friend…

- Have you tried the "Swish" pattern yet?
- Have you chosen your music? (Maybe more than one piece for different occasions.) Is one of them your phone's ringtone now?
- Have you tried mental rehearsal yet? It could be a simple as meeting new people and mentally rehearsing exactly how you want to behave.
- Have you chosen your role models and copied them? Perhaps imagine, too, being in a difficult situation and thinking, "What would my role model do here?"

CHAPTER **SIX**

Be your own best friend

Why would you argue for your limitations?

Here's a novel strategy for success: find out what works for you, and do that; notice what doesn't work, and don't do that. A little obvious, don't you think? And yet, is the following scenario familiar to you...

I have a friend who has always had a very difficult time dealing with other people. She was telling me about somebody who had asked her to do something she didn't want to do, but she went ahead and did it anyway. I asked her, "Why didn't you just say no?" And she replied, "Well, I couldn't do that. It's just me. It's just the way I am." So I said, "But how does that work for you?" "Well, it doesn't at all," she admitted. "So why don't you change something then?" I asked her, and she simply said, "Because it's just me. It's just the way I am." At that point I knew that was the end of the conversation.

I guess I'm not a very good person with whom to have that sort of conversation. In the past I've had the same attitude as my friend and all it did was make my life more difficult. Now I'm a bit like the former smoker who is more obsessively anti-smoking than someone who has never smoked at all. I've argued for my own limitations, and I know that the more family, friends or anyone else push you, the more you tend to defend your position with, "They just don't understand!"

To behave this way or not is something you have to decide for yourself. I've done the, "Oh, I'm shy" bit and the, "Oh, I can't speak in front of groups of people." Shy people are often drawn to horses because they feel it's an area where they can trust and not be judged, but, ironically, I knew

◁ *Love your horse, but be kind to yourself too.*

△ *Me answering questions during an Intelligent Horsemanship course.*

Sometimes it comes down to making a decision…

Around the time I was riding successfully in amateur races, I decided I needed to weigh up the pros and cons of my career and see whether I'd be better off doing something else. Although my race results were good, I was barely making enough money to live on. So, I decided I had two options:

OPTION 1: To continue to be very shy, live on starvation rations in horrible surroundings and eventually have to give up working with horses.

OPTION 2: Get over all the negativity and shyness and develop the personality I required to be a "Celebrity Guest Speaker" at the races. This new career would earn me really good money for simply chatting to people about horses.

Hmmm, which course would you have advised me to follow…?

However, I recognized that I needed help in making this change and so I found the name of a wonderful hypnotherapist, John Matthews (we're still in touch to this day). I remember how nervous I was before my first appointment with him; it's embarrassing to have to explain, "You see, I want to be able to talk to people…"

that if I wanted to spend my life around horses (which I did), meekly accepting such a persona and attitude to life was going to work against everything I wanted to do.

Tip the odds in your favor and "cheat"

Rather than accept the "shy" label and struggle on, I went for the easier option, which was to change and start to live the life that I wanted. Sometimes, though, you watch people and you can't help but think that they prefer to make life harder for themselves—this thought often occurs to me when I watch people handling horses. Many people make things as difficult as possible for themselves by not thinking things through, not having the right equipment ready and by not ensuring that everything is safe for themselves and their horses.

If one advances confidently in the direction of his dreams and endeavors to live the life he has imagined, he will meet with a success unexpected in common hours.

HENRY THOREAU

People have said to me, "It's so much easier for you starting young horses because you do it all in a round pen." And my answer is, "You are so *right*, it really helps a lot if the horse can't get loose and run away a few miles…" I've also been asked, "If your horse won't load and keeps stepping off the side of the ramp, isn't it cheating if you park by a fence so they can't run off the side?" Maybe, but what I want to know is, who is making these rules? So I happily tell people that if it's cheating, then at least it's cheating in favor of the horse.

When you are building confidence in your horse, yourself, or someone you are helping, I want you to remember another saying: "In the early stages you need to make it easy to do the right thing." Some bright spark might then ask, "So what happens if you have to load a horse on the side of the road?" Let's get this perfectly clear: you don't try loading your horse at the

Set yourself up for success

Here's a little lecture the students on my 5-day practical course receive before they start their journey home: it's all about setting yourself up for success.

First, I ask whether anyone who has been to a loading demonstration given by Monty or me has ever seen us fail to load the horse? (I think this is a good thing for them to think about, whether their journey is just a few miles or they have a flight home to Australia.) I know the answer is going to be "no" because it's never (yet) happened, so next I explore the reasons why this is the case.

Monty and I have both worked extremely hard to "master the art" of loading horses—communicating with the horse through the rope to his halter in such a way as to make it desirable for him to come forward. That's not just dragging on the rope (which would be more likely to make him want to go backwards), but using a technique of pressure and release to encourage the horse to come forward. Prior to that we have "Joined Up" (the special bonding technique we use) with the horse to begin to develop a relationship where the horse is far more likely to trust and want to be with us. Obviously, we ensure that the trailer we are using is safe and a suitable size for the horse with which we are working.

However, Monty and I know that even those things may not be enough to encourage a previously "unloadable" horse to load, so we always have various contingency plans for the initial training. (The aim, of course, is for the horse to eventually want to load with no problems at all, but here I'm talking about the initial stages of the process, where he may need more help to overcome a real phobia.) These tricks of the trade include using the Dually halter, a rope over 20 feet in length to hold him, and perhaps also easily maneuverable metal panels, which can be used as wings to help the horse find his way in. Not only this, I point out, but the fact is we are also surrounded by some of the best people *in the world* who know the work we do, and who are there at a moment's notice should we need a hand with anything.

▷ A happy owner can't believe that not only can Monty load her horse, but now she can too!

So now you are aware of this information – don't you think that, yes, we *should* be able to load any horse we are presented with? But, more to the point, don't you think *you* deserve an equal chance, too?

side of the road (or jumping your horse around a really high course or entering a dressage class) until the process is going effortlessly for both of you at home. When your horse learns to do something in one place, don't forget that he then has to learn to do it in other places and at other times so he (and you) become completely confident.

Give up on blame—it's an attitude that will work against you

I remember as a teenager listening to a woman in her fifties complaining about how she'd been held back all her life—I've forgotten the precise details, but perhaps it was because her mother said she had a big nose, her father made her watch *Morecombe and Wise* repeats and her sister gave her sour milk in her cereal. You know the sort of thing! As I listened to this I thought, "Well, the reason my life isn't going the way I want it to is because my mother/father/sister doesn't understand me, but I had no idea you would still be moaning about it when you were an *old* person." (You can be so harsh when you're young.)

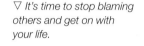

▽ *It's time to stop blaming others and get on with your life.*

Life, experience and observation have taught me that if you don't deal with the "monsters" from your past as soon as possible, then it doesn't just get better with time. In fact, I've seen cases where it gets a great deal worse as the person becomes more resentful. There is, without doubt, a case for coming to terms with your past, as much as you can, early on in life. I'm not saying you can't share your family history with a close friend or relative at an appropriate time, but a counselor might be more helpful in making sense of personal issues and bring closure to them. Which would you prefer: the life of your dreams, or a gravestone with, "It wasn't my fault my life was boring" written on it?

Countless memoirs and autobiographies relate tales of tough childhoods and terrible hardships, but in general these books have a positive message. In most cases there is a happy ending where the author has managed to make a good life for herself. The importance of the story here is how the author *overcame* the tough times, not dwelled on them and let them hold her back.

Someone did me a bad turn once and therefore I know how it feels to want to react by saying, "Why me? It's not fair!" But a friend gave me a wonderful piece of advice. He asked, "Do you know what the best revenge on nasty people is?" To which my reply was, "But I thought we'd decided that violence is never the answer?" And he said, "No, it's much more effective than that. The best revenge is to be happy. It is absolutely, without doubt, the best punishment for nasty people!" I've been living by that rule ever since, and it's one of the best pieces of advice that I've ever been given.

Make your life easier by appreciating how your horse thinks

To make it easy for your horse to do the right thing you've got to be able to appreciate how he thinks. Knowing this will give you an enormous advantage over the average person around horses. For instance, one thing to remember is that he always knows which direction his home or escape route is. This is not because he is "naughty"; this is because he's a flight animal who needs to look after himself. In the same way, if you find yourself in an unfamiliar area of a rough town you would be wise to work out your best route to safety, should any trouble arise.

So the first bit of "horse sense" you need is always to be aware of where the horse is most likely to be drawn to and then in your schooling, whether on the ground or ridden, you can keep this in mind and use it to your advantage. So if you are worried your horse might be a bit strong for you when you do a canter, make sure you canter *away* from the direction of home. If your horse is reluctant to load into the trailer, keep it open at the front so he can see his friends—don't try to lead him directly away from them. Once you start getting things right consistently, and you grow in confidence, then you can test yourself by making things a little bit more difficult. This way of thinking is all a part of the "be your own best friend" strategy—to make your life easier, not more difficult.

What would you rather do – learn, grow, explore and improve, or always look good?

Now, don't get me wrong – you're allowed to look good, you're even allowed to look fabulous as you hack out into the sunset, sail over those fences, ride that dressage test, give that talk. It's just that, while you are accruing the skills and abilities you need to get there, you might find yourself looking less than polished.

This is sometimes an issue on our foundation courses. Obviously people want to do the best they can, but sometimes this desire for it all to go "right" can actually make it more likely to go wrong, because they start worrying about how the horse is responding and what the tutor and other students are thinking about their performance. If everything doesn't go totally to plan, sometimes a student might feel they've failed in some way. But, this is the *foundation* course—it's where students come to learn the techniques, not to come and impress us by showing us they know everything.

So we always advise our students that if things don't go exactly to plan, they should welcome it as a learning opportunity. Instead of reacting with despair, "Oh no, this horse isn't reacting as he should. I've messed up. This is terrible," the student is advised to think, "Oh, great, an opportunity to work out what to do here. This could be really useful if this sort of situation ever comes up when I'm at home alone." Which attitude do you think is not only the most likely to make you learn and succeed, but also to enjoy learning along the way?

This is a good example of using every experience for your upliftment, learning and growth. It is such good advice. You might not enjoy every one of life's experiences, but try to separate yourself from your feelings of discomfort. These feelings are not you, they are just another experience you're going through.

If you have a negative feeling, just remember that this too will pass. If you're embarrassed about something, ask yourself, "Will this matter in ten years' time?" The most likely answer to this last question is that will be so insignificant you won't even remember it. Each time you feel uncomfortable, use it to help you learn something about yourself and it will lead you forward and let you grow.

This is a fantastic principle for life because it allows you to experience negative events and make them appear potentially positive. Instead of thinking, "Something terrible's happening to me; that's not how it should be," you can see the event as a challenge and an opportunity to grow and learn. Suddenly the "what-ifs" don't seem so frightening, and it's much easier to welcome the difficulties as part of life's rich tapestry. I guess the old-fashioned term for those sort of experiences would be "character-building"!

Helpful beliefs vs. unhelpful beliefs—introducing the placebo effect

The Latin word *placebo* means "I will please."

Numerous medical tests have proved that it's often enough simply to make a patient *believe* he is taking an effective pill—even though it may be made out of a substance with no medical value whatsoever. At a certain children's school I know, if ever a child grazes a knee or has a minor accident the "magic blue tissues" come out, and the child stops crying as they watch the magic tissue get to work.

This is where the placebo comes in. The power of the human brain is enormous; some people even argue that healing and various alternative remedies only work because the people taking them believe they will. It can be a hard task to convince a skeptic. I'm not interested in arguing either way in this case. However, what I would ask you to assess very carefully is, what are the *helpful beliefs* you have and what are the *unhelpful ones*?

The Kellsborough Lad story (opposite) turned out to be a very helpful belief for me, and it saw me through some tough times. It wouldn't have done me any favors to have someone come up and tell me that just because I was named after a horse that was brave, it didn't mean that I would be brave too. (Besides, the horse probably was just lucky enough to be a little bit faster and stronger than the others.) You can argue all you like, but I am always going to hold onto that belief as long as I find it's helpful to me.

Once again I'm not encouraging you to be delusional or unrealistic, it's just so important to be aware of how powerfully our beliefs can affect our performance—so we might as well try to use the helpful ones. Studies have shown that those who expect the best often get the best—this is the "Pygmalion effect," or the "teacher-expectancy effect." This effect is shown in situations in which certain students perform better than others simply because they are expected to do so; and if the teachers were led to expect a better performance from particular children, then their level of improvement could be about twice that of other children in the same class. Thus this revealed that biased expectancies can essentially affect real situations and create self-fulfilling prophecies as a result. So, be biased in favor of yourself!

A horse called Kellsborough Lad

I was born on 1 January (the official birthday for racehorses) and named Kelly after a horse my father trained—Kellsborough Lad. I knew this but I didn't hear the full story until I was almost 7.

When I was about 6 years old I became really frightened of going to school (there was a nun, I remember, who terrified me; I was also bemused by "colorfactor" arithmetic lessons). Anyway, one night I was in bed crying about going to school. I think Mom sent Dad up to "talk to me"; he came in and didn't even ask what I was crying about. He just said, "Do you know why you were called Kelly?" I didn't, so he said, "Because you were named after the bravest horse I ever had. Kellsborough Lad won 17 jump races and he was very strong and very brave and he always did the very best he could." And that was it; he went downstairs again.

Weirdly, this was enough to make me feel better. Somehow I understood that "we Kellys" possessed an inner strength and bravery. It got me through that time and funnily enough, some 20 years later, as I was sobbing about something (nothing to do with nuns or colorfactor this time), the memory of that night suddenly came back to me. I remembered what Dad had said about Kellsborough Lad—that he was strong and brave and always tried his best—and again it changed my attitude to whatever was upsetting me. From then on, I knew I could handle whatever life threw at me.

This story isn't to tell you about me, though, or even about my dad or Kellsborough Lad; it's to remind us how important, and even life-changing, the things we say to children (and to adults) can be. Have you ever told someone something that might change their life? Could you find a genuine compliment to give someone this week? Don't save it for their funeral.

I used to find this approach really difficult, as it wasn't something I was brought up to do. But it's like anything else you do: the more you practice the easier it gets. So now I want you to think of the best thing that anyone ever said to you when you were growing up (you're only allowed to think of the good things!). If you can't remember any uplifting comments, you're allowed to make up something—what would you have liked someone to have said to you when you were 7 years old and scared? Remember the subconscious mind very often can't tell the difference between reality and fiction, so choose any message you'd like, from whoever you'd like and make it yours to keep forever. Then think, what would you like to hear now? Here are some examples, if you haven't got your own ideas. As you go to sleep imagine your granny saying, "We're always so proud of you," and believe it. Or imagine your father saying, "There was always something special about you," and believe it. Or imagine your mother saying, "We always knew you were strong enough to handle anything," and believe it.

Examples of helpful or unhelpful beliefs you might have

Unhelpful belief: "My horse tries to make a fool of me." If you are silly enough to believe something like this then maybe you deserve that kind of horse! Horses don't plot or scheme (as humans do), so this is an unhelpful belief because it stops you trying to work out the real reasons behind your horse's behavior, and thereby find a way to improve things between you.

How we believe the world is and what we honestly think it can become have powerful effects on how things turn out.

JAMES RHEM, EXECUTIVE EDITOR,

NATIONAL TEACHING AND LEARNING FORUM

Helpful belief: "My horse is always trying his best for me." Believing the best of your horse and putting you both on the same team means you'll keep finding the good in each other.

Unhelpful belief: "I'll never make a rider because I started riding too late." This is obviously an unhelpful belief because it will harm your motivation and such things can become self-fulfilling prophecies. Find out about good riders who started later in life—there are hundreds of examples.

Helpful belief: "I might have started riding later, but every day in every way I'm getting better and better. I'm more aware and in control of my body than I was when I was younger, and I've developed a lot of useful learning strategies that will accelerate my improvement"—that's more like it!

Don't believe horses can read your mind!

In *Become Perfect Partners* we looked at the "mirror, mirror in the stall"—how the way we feel about ourselves can be "mirrored" in horses and can affect them, for better or for worse.

Our inner state is definitely a really important thing to explore if we want to improve our horsemanship (and our lives). However, can horses, as some people suggest, really read our minds? Do you have to be spiritually pure to be able to have a really good bonding session? Is your every thought and feeling completely transparent to your horse? But, most importantly, is this a helpful belief? It is if you take time to notice how you're feeling before working with a horse, and then keep checking in to see if something you're doing could be affecting the horse's behavior. It's not a helpful belief if you spend the whole time you're with your horse thinking, "Oh my goodness, he knows how nervous I am and it must be really upsetting him!" That approach really isn't doing either of you any favors.

So, take it from me that if you act as if you are completely confident then your horse will respond in the same way. How can I be so sure? Because I've ridden in competition when I've been shaking with anticipation, but from the start I acted as if I were a brave, confident rider, and enjoyed the best results in my life. I've still got my name in the British Show Jumping Association Championship Year Book to prove I "fooled" the horse (and myself!) on more than one occasion. Just watch any top performer in action; when something is really important to them they go into what's known as "the zone." This is where they shut out the outside world and they just "know" what they have to achieve. Personally, I think horses love it when a handler or rider practices this with them: they suddenly feel totally focused, safe and protected. It must be so reassuring to know "your human" is not someone to be messed with!

Even Monty, who's done demonstration after demonstration with "horses with problems," has had days when, for one reason or another he's been upset, annoyed, depressed

ASSIGNMENT
Belief

Write down now what you "know" about your riding and divide your thoughts between the "helpful" or "unhelpful" categories. Look at your list and resolve to change all your beliefs to helpful ones.

or simply tired (he's only human, after all!). I remember at Hartpury College, moments before he went in to the arena to do his demonstration, someone told Monty that the Queen Mother had died. He was very fond of, as well as grateful to, the Queen Mother for the kindness she had shown him in the past, and I could see his eyes well up with tears as he went out. But did the horses all refuse to cooperate or respond to his methods because they could "sense" something was wrong? This is where professionalism comes in—an attitude whereby you give your best to the job at hand every single day, whatever the circumstances.

The difference between the person living their dreams and the one who isn't is that the former is not busy making excuses—she's busy getting on with what she's got to do to make things work.

Others are relying on you—be brave for their sake

If you were an adult looking after a 3-year-old child and you thought there was a burglar in the house, I know that you would act bravely to protect the child. You might say, "Let's play a game now where you hide under the bed and keep very, very quiet while I pretend to call the police." You'd probably surprise yourself with this response, because we don't realize that we all possess the strength to be brave enough at a time when we really need to be.

The trouble is, thankfully, that most of us won't often find ourselves in a situation where we can test this theory. Life can be pretty mundane and it's easy to get stuck in a rut when you don't do anything that takes you out of your comfort zone. Think of a time when you surprised yourself

Facing fear

I have always admired horses from afar, but I've also always been afraid of them. My daughter Gemma recently bought her own horse (a big, beautiful thoroughbred cross called Indi), but it wasn't long before my enthusiasm paled to sheer fear. I spent the first year backing away from Indi and I only managed to groom him a little. Eventually, frustrated by the lack of hands-on support I could offer Gemma, and having already watched her successfully complete the Intelligent Horsemanship Five-Day Foundation Course, I decided to have a go myself.

On the first day I arrived after a night of little sleep and had even broken out in a nervous rash, but for my daughter's sake I couldn't pull out. As I waited for my first Join Up, the old familiar heart-pounding, dizzy, sick feeling kicked in. My tutor, Linda Ruffle, asked me if I'd like to work with Indi. I felt that he'd been inviting me to get near to him for some time now, so I told her it felt right. I remembered Kelly saying to me, "When you're not confident, act as if you are," and from somewhere I found enough courage to have a successful Join Up.

The following day went well, too, but then came the real turning point. Waiting for my turn I saw what looked like a large, strong horse being led into the round pen. He was agitated, and to my mind ill-mannered. I was terrified, but I went in and took the lead rope. Soon he was trotting round and I began to feel out of my depth, so I asked Linda to come and take the rope while I pulled myself together. I was trembling from head to foot, thinking how vulnerable I was. Linda explained that the horse, Joe, didn't have any bad intentions; he had been bullied and was nervous of people. He'd come on the course to get good experiences with humans. I suddenly realized that it was my choice: I could either live my life in fear, or earn self-respect by facing that fear and overcoming it. I returned to Linda and Joe and said I was ready.

Back in the pen I was conscious of Joe kicking and bucking, rushing or cutting in on the circle. It was just me and Joe; eyes on eyes, shoulders square. I knew I couldn't back down now. Eventually he settled down and I invited him for the Join Up. As I stood there, stroking him between the eyes, he relaxed and gave a big sigh. I was suddenly aware that *he* had been fearful and unsure and that this process wasn't all about me. It was a revelation.

Joe was a great teacher, coming into my life at just the right time. He made me realize that fear itself is worse than the actual cause of that fear, and by understanding this we can face it and conquer its self-destructive pattern.

HELEN KERRIGAN

with how brave you were. Relive the story; tell a friend. The courage to face difficult situations was there when you needed it and it's there every day, but you need to push yourself. Do something that makes you the teeniest bit uncomfortable every day (or at least every few days).

How have you stretched your comfort zone this week? What little thing did you want to resist, but you did it anyway and now you feel pretty pleased with yourself? Stretching your comfort zone will work for you in many different ways, and it doesn't all have to be horse-related. Start a conversation with the new person at your barn/the show, or arrange to meet up with the friends you make at the Intelligent Horsemanship Discussion Group. (There is even a special confidence section!) Don't tell me you're shy—we're all shy!

Anyway, getting back to the plot, you know you can be brave if someone needs protecting, so:

- Be brave for the sake of your horse – reassure him that things are going to be all right.
- Be brave for the sake of the other people around you who want to enjoy their horses and their riding.
- Be brave for the sake of any children around you, so they don't pick up your anxiety and become anxious adults.

Putting yourself in the role of being confident will help you to help others—either other people or your horse. Being able to do this is about self-image again. Sometimes it acceptable to lean on others, but even the staunchest of friends will start to be less than impressed if you take your feet off the ground and fasten yourself around their neck.

Sometimes you need to be there for others, but can you step up to the task? Here are two stories of people who did just that.

Build good self-image with bold challenges

What brave people do is to build positive "reference experiences" by having a go at something that takes them out of their comfort zones. They can look back at these achievements whenever they are feeling doubtful and remember, "I was the person who went into the pen and helped that challenging horse," or "I helped a friend overcome her trail riding fears, even though I'd been frightened myself."

The best "positive reference experiences" are those that are truly frightening but involve almost no actual risk. Perhaps you would feel fantastic about yourself if you went clear around Rolex, but if you've never attempted a hunter course it's probably not a good idea. A popular one with Tony Robbins, the "guru" of personal development, is the "firewalk." Walking over 10 yards of burning-hot coals is an extraordinary experience.

CASE STUDY

Setting a good example

I gave up riding and horses for nearly 10 years after a frightening collision on the road. Neither my horse of that time nor I were injured, but I totally lost my confidence and stopped riding. Two years ago I got a new horse, Lincoln. (I cried all night because I couldn't believe what I'd done. Getting another horse – what on earth was I thinking of?) It has taken me quite some time to build up my confidence on him. Reading Kelly's books has really helped.

I've recently met another rider and I'm having to be the brave, confident one as she is new to riding. She hasn't ridden on the road yet as she is too nervous, although her horse is very steady, but we want to hack out to different places and so it is essential to negotiate some roads. So now I am helping her as my horse is very reliable on the road. Our goal is to meet up with some others from a nearby barn, as they have some rides we don't know.

This morning, a windy day, we went for a little hack along a road near us. We had planned to go further afield but the wind and rain were against us, so we decided just to do a short stretch of road between two bridlepaths. We were very safety-conscious in our high-visibility riding gear and the horses were so good. I told my friend to sing (in her head) if she got worried, as I know it helps for me! (I even sing out loud, if I am forgetting to breathe.)

We were absolutely fine. What good, brave horses we have! I left my friend at her barn and on the way home I met a huge tractor and trailer and, again, my horse was perfect.

I'm now sitting here with my hot chocolate, beaming and thinking, isn't it funny: I am now so busy trying to give my friend confidence that my own lack of confidence has been forgotten!

JUDITH GLEASE

Sober dress to sturdy boots

You'd think someone who was a lawyer would have all the confidence in the world. I joined the Courts' Service because I was worried about public speaking, but little did I appreciate that I would spend the next 20 years sitting in open court, directing proceedings, advising magistrates, unravelling problems and dealing with confrontation and deep emotions! I loved all of that—it was the bureaucracy that brought me down.

My life as an Intelligent Horsemanship Recommended Associate, where I help owners and horses to understand each other better, is very similar: I direct the horses, advise the owners, unravel problems and deal with confrontation and deep emotions. However, now I am hidden away on a farm in the New Forest and public appearances are much rarer. Recently, though, I undertook an informal demonstration at the Margaret Green Foundation Trust in Dorset. Over 200 people came and watched me. I found myself fumbling with a girth and my adrenalin levels were very high, so I took a deep breath, remembered that I needed to be there for the horse and began to smile. Knowing that my message was greater than my fear enabled me to do the best I could for the horse, the audience and myself.

SARAH WESTON, INTELLIGENT HORSEMANSHIP RECOMMENDED ASSOCIATE

The idea is that you're actually pretty safe (due to some little-known law of thermodynamics), but you're still really frightened. So even though people know they are safe, you would still expect them to feel "stretched," with a pumping heart, dry mouth and sweaty palms.

That's the point. That's how these experiences build your confidence —you feel the fear, you do it anyway and, later, when you're feeling insecure, you look back on them and remind yourself, "Of course I can do this, I've done the firewalk!" Having done the firewalk I think that we horsepeople (that's you and I) are going to find it far easier to face it than people in many other walks of life who have never had to face anything remotely physically challenging. Never mind riding horses, going out in all weathers just to *do* things for our horses takes an enormous amount of determination and tenacity—non-horse people think we're mad! So let's appreciate just how tough we really are.

Keep your promises!

This may sound like a strange technique for developing confidence, but it's pretty much guaranteed to work. Think of your brain as a big monitoring device: not only does it regulate things like body temperature and heart rate, it also constantly scans your world for things that you and others around you say, do and believe, and then tries to make sense of it all.

Your brain will quite happily ignore "facts" that don't fit in with its developing theories and search for those that do. It continually compares and contrasts what is expected to happen with what actually does, so that it can continue to refine its assessment. So when it hears you say, "I'm going to ride at 6 o'clock tomorrow morning," and then you turn your alarm clock off without even waking up, your brain makes a little note along the lines of "Early morning riding promises don't always come true." If you then break these promises to yourself a few times, your brain modifies its note to "Early morning riding plans almost NEVER happen." Then your brain will help you to fulfil this state of affairs and assist you in coming up with even more reasons NOT to go riding.

Perhaps this wouldn't be the biggest problem if the only consequence of this was your horse's resulting lack of fitness, but it's more far-reaching than that. Saying that you'll do things that you then don't—whether they're promises to yourself or to others—creates doubt in your own ability to see things through. When you say, "I AM going to ride that horse tomorrow," there's a part of your awareness that says, "Really? I'll believe it when I see it." You may feel absolutely convinced about what you are going to do, but part of you still doubts it. And, depressing though it may feel, there's a part of you that, when you do find an excuse not to ride, feels a sense of "rightness" because this fits into what you were expecting. As you break more and more promises to yourself and others you get more and more demoralized about your sense of worth. Then, when that promotion comes up for grabs, or someone offers you a great job or there's a fabulous horse to ride, you're wracked with self-doubt because you know that you're fundamentally unreliable.

Luckily, the solution is simple: just do what you say you're going to do. This is much easier to achieve if you're very realistic about what you take on. Only make commitments that you know you can keep. To gain mental strength the best idea I know of is to make only one very small, doable commitment a day. Then, when you've achieved that for 21 days and you start to see yourself as a person who *does* follow through on her promises, you can think about being a little more ambitious!

Encourage others to support you in your efforts; if someone asks you to do something for them they'll need to understand you can't do it because you have this other commitment. Someone asks you out to dinner? Great, but it'll have to be a late sitting because you're riding in the early evening. Don't really feel like it? That's no excuse at all; you've made a commitment now and that feeling will go once you've started, and think of how much better you're going to feel as a trustworthy person who can follow through on her pledges… I promise you, keeping your promises will make an impression on every single area of your life.

▽ Keep your promises! If you say you're going to ride at 5:00 A.M., then ride at 5:00 A.M.

Throw your hat over the wall

Miles Hilton Barber— the blind explorer-extraordinaire whose many achievements include climbing Kilimanjaro and completing the grueling Marathon des Sables—suggests that when you want to achieve something big you commit to it by "throwing your hat over the wall." This idea relates to a time when, as a boy, he wanted to skip school and snag some apples from an orchard. The wall was high and he and his friend couldn't see over it, but suddenly his friend took off his cap and threw it far over the wall. "Are you mad?" Miles exclaimed. "We'll get in so much trouble when they find out we've missed school and lost your cap!" "Well, we'll just have to find some way of getting it back then," his friend replied. And they did.

▽ *Once committed to the demonstrations we had to keep up our practice without a wobble.*

We can use different variations of this technique. For instance, I had been meaning to do a few of my own demonstrations with Pie because I thought it would give us both something challenging to aim for, a reason to get fit and because, in spite of all the organization needed to make one happen, they are great fun when you're there on the night. However in 2006, with so many course commitments, work at home, one thing and another (excuses, excuses), it didn't happen. Then 2007 came around and looked even more busy. Now, remember this was something I *wanted* to do, not *had* to do, and I wanted to do it because it would mean I would have to make Pie and my exercise a priority, rather than always having something "more important" to do. So I used the technique of "making it happen so you can't back out": I booked the venues where the demonstrations were to be held in five months' time, had the tickets printed and advertised the demonstrations on our website. This really works—it's a real motivator.

Alternatively you could make a commitment to your "success buddy" (see chapter 4) and they could help in this way too. Agree to meet them at a certain time; if you aren't great at getting up early this may be the only way you'll ever get those morning runs or rides to happen. An early morning start makes it much more likely that you will be able to fulfil that commitment before your day becomes complicated and full of other commitments. Plus, you can then be smug all day and tackle anything that comes up, knowing that you've already ridden, or gone running or studied for an hour, or whatever it is you'd decided to do.

Make this something you can easily achieve: going out for a 20-minute walk every other day is something you can do even if you're not feeling on top form. Build on small successes and congratulate yourself unashamedly when you do it. Make sure your monitoring brain really notices that you did what you said you would do. Keep telling yourself and your success buddy: "Well done

▽ *"Do the thing you fear to do and keep on doing it… that is the quickest and surest way ever yet discovered to conquer fear." Dale Carnegie*

us! How good was that? Brilliant." Email, text or phone each other throughout the day, reminding each other how virtuous you were to accomplish that task this morning, last night or whenever it was you did it. If your success buddy doesn't want to go running or doesn't ride, they can still perform a helpful role as you can tell them your planned schedule, inform them when you've done things and ask them to check up on you too—and you can do the same for them with their tasks. Much cheaper than a life coach!

Develop a thicker skin!

It's interesting that worrying about what other people think seems to scare as many people as physical danger when they are dealing with their horses. If you start to take too seriously what other people think, you will pretty soon stop doing anything. Let's look at the "official" statistics—13.5 percent of people don't think at all; 38.4 percent of people, if they are thinking, aren't thinking about you anyway; and 46.3 percent of people are just so relieved it's not them on the spot that they either sympathize completely or else are simply happy to "live and let live." The remaining 1.8 percent of people are plain miserable and, yes, may even make a horrible remark. My, oh my, will you survive *that*?

In fact there are remarkable statistics (which are never wrong) that show that 100 percent of people *do* survive sarcastic comments. Nasty remarks such as, "People are laughing at her, she's making such a fool of herself," actually reflect the fears of the people making these comments. You should feel sorry for them, in truth, and we certainly don't want to live our lives to please *them*. How crazy would that be?

Every year thousands of men and women die of embarrassment—and I mean literally die of embarrassment—by not wanting to talk to their doctor about a problem in an intimate area. Embarrassment can not only hold us back enormously in life, it can even take our life. If this is your problem, I want you to think about this. If you want to override the discomfort you feel in certain situations, such as when asking for something at the pharmacy or riding in front of others, concentrate on the job in hand, get on with it and practice. Note how you feel afterwards: proud and happy? You did it! Congratulate yourself. Every time you don't let others control your behavior you'll find it a little bit easier.

Ignoring what other people think becomes much easier with maturity. Something that would have made you curl up with embarrassment when young is far less of an issue as you get older. I love the way that my mom, in her seventies, is on chatty terms with all the Olympic rowers and coaches when walking her dog, Luca, along the river at Henley, whereas younger people might rehearse conversations in their heads. "Oh, there's an Olympic rower/showjumper/event rider. I'd love to talk to them, but what would I say? They'll think I'm really stupid and that I'm just talking to them because of what they do (which I do really), or worse, that I fancy them. How embarrassing? So it's better to ignore them and not smile… and they're probably really big-headed and a real snob who will look down on me. How dare they? I hate them…" You know the kind of thing I mean!

So since I am as guilty of excessive thinking as anyone, I think I can offer some good first-hand advice. When I admitted to myself that being able to speak in public was going to help me live the life I wanted, my lovely hypnotherapist mentor gave me the idea of starting with small steps. He advised me to put my name on the Women's Institute speakers' list. Soon I was off to every borough in Berkshire, giving talks on my experiences as a lady jockey. They seemed to be quite grateful to hear a talk that differed from the more usual cake baking or macrame for beginners (you'll understand what I'm talking about if you've ever seen the film *Calender Girls*!).

If ever you are nervous about having to "perform" in front of people, the number-one rule is that you do *not* allow your imagination to run wild with worry about what they think about you. Remember those helpful versus unhelpful beliefs? "They're all out to get me and they're going to hate what I have to say" definitely falls under the unhelpful category. Fill your mind with positive thoughts. Be aware that you have to project your voice and use eye contact right around the room. As in "being brave for others' sakes," I know that in those circumstances I have to stop thinking about myself and imagine there is one person in the room who can really benefit from what I have to say. Then I can work as hard and as sincerely as I can to impart that information and entertain that one person in my mind. If I am riding a horse in front of people I put all the emphasis on my work with the horse and whether he is all right. The fact is that shyness, lack of confidence and fearfulness all take a great deal of concentration *on oneself*. The sooner you can take the emphasis off yourself and put it onto caring about *others*, the sooner you'll find that there isn't a problem at all.

Finding a mentor—can it change your life? (Yes!)

If you are lucky enough to find someone you really admire and aspire to emulate, you could be really smart and ask them to mentor you. Acquiring the right mentor is one of the very best ways of getting ahead in anything you want to do—you only have to read a few autobiographies to see the proof of that.

A mentor just means an experienced and trusted advisor, and it's probably not advisable to rush up to them saying, "Please be my mentor!" We have to be more subtle than that. But, do not be afraid, I'm sure we can devise a cunning plan to help you here… I have a story about a child against whom I used to compete. He didn't seem to receive much support from his parents (and I seem to remember him falling off his pony, Hankie Pankie, an awful lot). When the boy left school he turned up at the stable of showjumpers Ted and Liz Edgar and started working there, doing any job he was given. Within a few years the child had metamorphosized into Nick Skelton, the brilliant international showjumper.

▽ A mentor: someone whose hindsight can become your foresight.

My own mentor story, of meeting Monty, has similarities to this. I like to think of the phrase, "when the student is ready, the teacher will appear." Rather bizarrely, I met Monty in a gas station in France! I am fully aware of how lucky (and spooky!) this was; he must have met an awful lot of people in an awful lot of gas stations before, but probably no one as ready to hit the ground running as I was at that time. As soon as I realized that this was the missing link I'd been looking for in my horsemanship I organized my life around his visits to England so that I could help him work with remedial horses. I also worked on the manuscript for his book.

△ Me with my mentor, Monty Roberts.

I never at any stage asked for payment. I've found that, if you stick around for long enough and make yourself as useful as possible (otherwise you're just a nuisance), after a while people start to feel *responsible* for you. (This is letting you into a secret, and it's a trick that has since worked on me!) As a mentor myself, I often feel guilty about letting people work for nothing, "that's not really fair, I must pay them *something*." This stage is called, in old-fashioned terms, "Getting your feet under the table," After this stage the mentor is suddenly taken by surprise because the mentee

Luck is preparation meeting opportunity

has by now become very, very good at the job they took over. In fact, they have become the best person. So I might panic as I realize that they are now indispensable—how could I ever replace them?

Meanwhile, this person has taken a short cut into all my knowledge and can avoid making the mistakes I made. Instead he or she can get on the fast track to better and brighter things. I believe that, just as with your own children, a measure of your success is the fact that these "mentees" are able to fly the nest and go on to succeed on their own merits (although I have to admit that having my mentees around is lovely and rewarding too).

One of the things to think about when seeking out a mentor is that it's helpful to have one or two skills to offer them before you start. So if you're young, start developing some key skills as early as you can. When I met Monty it made all the difference that I could drive, was a "good hand around horses" (as he called me) and I could read and type at speed. Later on it also proved useful that I'd already done some teaching and could write effective advertising headlines. If you're not so young and reading this, but throughout your life you've picked up a weird mix of skills, you may find it interesting that there might come a time in your life when they suddenly all fit together and make sense.

Since I'm virtually your mentor now, I must be completely honest and advise you that, however lovely and selfless the mentor you have your eye on appears, they are very likely to have some degree of ego and will be interested in what you can do for *them*. We receive many job applications and work experience requests at the Intelligent Horsemanship office during the year. Some of them start with no "Dear" anyone and then go on "iam studyng my ecquine degee and do you have any jobs goin? Tanya." A big contrast to the beautifully written letter I received from our now youngest Recommended Associate Rosie Jones (I've still got it for sentimental reasons) and not only does she list all that *she could do for Intelligent Horsemanship,* rather than the normal list of what the person wants us to do for them, but I couldn't help smiling when I read the line "I would love the opportunity to work for, and learn from, you because I think to be the best I can, I should learn from the best." Anyone in any doubt as to why I decided immediately that this must be a very intelligent and talented young lady?!

Be around uplifting people

Have you ever found that being around certain people inspires you and gives you more energy, whereas other people can be energy drainers? If you have someone in your life that always bring your mood down and makes your confidence in life ebb away, I think you know what to do (now that you're your own best friend).

Spend time with people who support and energize you and, yes, this may mean you need to change your friends and/or your environment if you recognize that someone is not on your side. This is not to suggest that you should surround yourself with people who'll say everything you do is great when it's not, but rather those who might sit you down and say, "I've been worried about some of the things you're doing lately and I'd really like to talk…" They shouldn't be downbeat on life; they should be give-it-

100-percent-type people. They've got plans; they know how to have fun and they want you to have fun, and they are ready to support your plans just as you're prepared to support theirs.

Life strategies

We don't get any official training in life strategies: we might learn history and computer skills at school, but none of the important stuff, such as how to get on with others, what makes some people likely to live the life of their dreams and why others work against themselves all their lives. You have to figure things out for yourself: sometimes it can take 20 years or more, and sometimes people never get it. What an awful thought!

As Dr. Phil McGraw (celebrity psychologist and best-selling author) says, "Life gives you clues," but how can we be sure we're more Sherlock Holmes than Watson? It's so easy to recognize in another person that they are making the same mistake over and over again, and we can see a mile off when other people are about to make a ridiculous decision. And yet

▽ *Life's more fun spent around upbeat people who are heading in the same direction as you.*

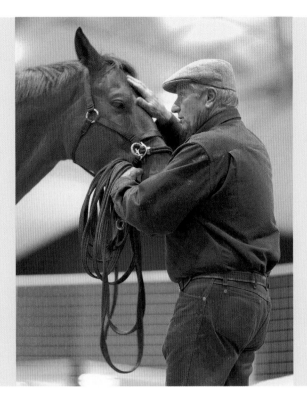

*A good horseman can hear
a horse talk.
A great horseman can hear
a horse whisper.*

MONTY ROBERTS

we think our decisions are so well thought out and rational we've no idea how we ever get anything wrong—perhaps we're just "unlucky" at times?

A good way to test if you've been reading life's clues is to look at the situation you're in *right now* and just suppose, for the sake of this exercise, that everything about your life at the moment is the result of decisions you took in the last few weeks, months or years. How well are you riding —right now? How knowledgeable are you about horses—right now? If you had taken the decision to go on some courses or planned a program of extra study 5 years ago would things be different now? How fit are you and your horse? If you had planned 3 months ago for you both to get fit together, would things be different—right now? How do you and your horse perform at shows? If you had made different decisions in the past —i.e. taken that educational course, not eaten that cheese cake—how could things be different now? I'm not talking about having regrets for the past, but if you can understand more about how you got to where you are now (good or bad), then this can help you decide how to make decisions that are going to get you to where you want to be in the future.

This exercise can be so helpful to you if you follow it through. By being quite hard on yourself initially it's ultimately very positive for you to understand that, if you want to be living differently in the future, you need to make the changes *now*—not sit around waiting for things to happen. If you don't think that you're currently on the path to achieving your dreams, could it be that you have been missing the clues that life has been sending you? You have to acknowledge that the majority of situations don't just happen overnight. A good example of this is one of Monty's favorite phrases to quote—"Suddenly—for no reason at all—he just went crazy!" Did this "going crazy" really come out of nowhere, do you think? Or are there people who have been missing the clues their horse (and life) has been giving them over and over again?

Checklist

Have you:

- worked out any additional qualities you need and "who you've got to be" in order to achieve your dreams and goals?
- given up blaming others and started taking responsibility for your life?
- given up trying to be perfect and just keep praising yourself for every little improvement you make?
- identified your helpful beliefs? And your unhelpful beliefs?
- stretched your comfort zone even just a little bit recently?
  You felt uncomfortable, but you did it anyway…
- thought about in what ways are you setting yourself up for success?
- thought of times you have been, or could be, brave for others?
- been keeping your promises to others? And to yourself?
- made a commitment for success by promising to do something at a definite date in the future?
- found your mentor yet?
- been working on your support team? How many members does it have now?
- analyzed the clues life has been giving you?
  What are your conclusions?

CHAPTER **SEVEN**

No more excuses!

THE ULTIMATE "LETTING GO" EXERCISE

Sometimes, although we really believe we want to do something (such as hack out on our own or drive a horsebox) or to *stop* doing something (say, overeating or overspending), we still carry on with self-defeating behaviors —much to the puzzlement of ourselves and our nearest and dearest. In fact, we often make up good reasons to try to convince ourselves that, "I can't help myself/I'm not responsible."

Perhaps you are right; perhaps you see other people doing quite regular things—like hacking out their horse, keeping their stable tidy or driving a horse trailer—and, although they don't seem that different to you, perhaps there is just a malfunction in your brain that means that you will never be able to work towards developing those skills. But don't you think that's a bit unlikely?

Often we hang onto our "it's just me" attitude because it does give you an unconscious pay-off. If you've been aware of this you might have considered getting professional help to see why you've been holding yourself back, but then talked yourself out of doing it by saying you haven't got the time or the money, or you don't know who to appproach.

◁ *Pie and Daisy jumping to win the Desert Orchid Working Hunter class at Peterborough Championships.*

If you're not having fun when you're working with your horses, you need to change something.

MONTY ROBERTS

EXERCISE:
Self-image

You should be aware that we always (unless we make a conscious decision otherwise) act consistently with our self-image. Your self-image could be described as "who you believe you are."

Jot down now how you see yourself at the present time. What are your 10 greatest strengths? Write them down and take a moment to feel satisfied with yourself.

Now work out what it is that might be holding you back from being a confident rider; perhaps you already have a few ideas? The exercise opposite has proved life-changing to many of the people who have used it, and you can apply it to many different areas of your life.

We can always find excuses—but not in this book! There are other exercises within these pages that will help you tackle genuine fear and phobias, but this next one is intended to help you find out if there are other reasons that are holding you back that you haven't previously been aware of. Perhaps you can use this exercise to examine why you haven't sought professional help yet, if, as you claim, you really want to change so much!

Steering my life (and the horse trailer!)

Let's demonstrate with a simple, not too emotionally charged example, of how this exercise might work.

My own particular issue has been driving my horse trailer. I have owned a horse trailer for over 7 years but I have never driven it. Why not? Because,

EXERCISE:
Letting go!

Take a big piece of paper and choose a statement that you might say as a positive affirmation. Start it with, "I am now willing to…" Now fill in something reasonably specific. For example: "I am now willing to lose that last 10 pounds/be on time/take more time off," or "I am now willing to be a confident rider and hack my horse out/do a hunter trials/compete at such-and-such a level/ride a particular horse."

This statement can be anything that you really want to do. For instance, if there had been a fairy with a magic wand inside this book when you opened it (and there is!), what would you have told her you wanted to change? Because of the title of the book, I'm going to predict that it's something to do with your confidence around horses, but don't forget that this exercise can apply to many areas.

Using the same piece of paper, rewrite your "willing statement" on the left-hand side. To the right of that, write the first objection that springs to mind. Then write your willing statement again (this is the main reason you don't want it to be too long and involved), and after it write the next objection that occurs. Don't censor anything; just write it down. If you get stuck, make a cup of tea and come back later.

Expect to come up with around 20 objections; perhaps 30; maybe even 50. Keep going until you can't think of anything else to add. Your answers might start to seem quite bizarre, silly even, but you need to allow yourself that because that's when you're most likely to reach the breakthrough! Write down at least 15 reasons—however ridiculous they may seem—and if you can't think of one, then make it up!

When you're absolutely sure you've written down everything you can think of, go away for half an hour or so, then come back, settle down and take a look at the list. Some of the items may have caused "a-ha!" moments (you've probably seen these in a horse when he suddenly "gets" it; but we're that intelligent too!). Others may have puzzled you even as you were writing them down; some may appear as if you were being sarcastic and some might be very obvious. Take careful note of the ones that seem a bit silly, that defy logic or that would be really hard (even embarrassing) to explain to someone else; even if something looks irrational it doesn't mean it isn't exerting a powerful influence on your behavior.

"I don't drive the horse trailer." Sometimes people make statements like this in quite an aggressive or arrogant tone that defies you to question them; however, my excuse (which I genuinely believed at the time) was that I was nervous of driving the horse trailer because I might injure a lot of people if I had an accident.

Sounds reasonable, don't you think? No one had ever questioned it until one day I was telling a lady about my reluctance to drive the horse trailer. She was quite a bossy type—she clearly didn't suffer fools gladly. She just looked at me as though I was quite crazy and said, "Well, how ridiculous!" (Everything she says has an exclamation mark on the end.) "I've always thought of you as a person who was perfectly capable of doing anything they put their mind to!" And I felt a bit embarrassed, like my cover had been blown.

A short time after this, a situation arose where a friend needed help transporting a horse and there were none of the usual people around to do it. As we were calling around frantically to find someone to drive the horse trailer, it occurred to me, "This really is a bit ridiculous." In the absence of other people my reluctance to drive could no longer be dismissed as a "harmless indulgence." It now occurred to me that if one of our horses had to be taken to the vet's quickly and I couldn't drive the trailer, there would be no harmless indulgence involved in that.

Suddenly I had a real reason for wanting to change—and at once I understood why it is that people can give up smoking when they're pregnant or have survived a heart attack. I thought it would be interesting to explore whether it was *really* because I didn't think I'd be capable as a driver, or whether there might be other issues going on?

Here are just a few examples of the thought processes I went through:

- I am now willing to drive the horse trailer. I am not willing to drive the horse trailer because it's a stupid thing to do. (This is an example of a not particularly helpful answer, but getting beyond such childish answers is all part of the process.)
- I am now willing to drive the horse trailer. I am not willing to drive the horse trailer because I don't want to be a trailer driver living off bacon sandwiches and getting really unfit. (This one is clearly an excuse—I'm always "saying" I want to get fitter. Clearly, I need to go through this process for "I am now willing to get fit" as well!)

- I am now willing to drive the horse trailer. I am not willing to drive the horse trailer because once people know I can drive it I'll have to do it all the time. (This isn't valid because I am able to set boundaries in other areas of my life, so why wouldn't I be able to do so here?)
- I am now willing to drive the horse trailer. I am not willing to drive the horse trailer because once I do I'll have to go to shows and demonstrations on my own and what would be the fun of that? (Hmmm, now it's getting closer to some of my real concerns…)

As I started the process of changing my attitude towards the horse trailer, I began to question how I'd actually feel driving it—would I feel independent, successful, strong? In fact, when I honestly explored the meaning of driving the horse trailer I felt the complete opposite; as if I was a complete failure! If it's good enough for Princess Haya of Jordan and the Princess Royal, then why wouldn't it be good enough for me?

As I kept questioning why I didn't want to drive the trailer, some extraordinary thoughts started to occur: it's always been great fun to go off in a group in the horse trailer; if I drove it myself would I now have to go off on my own? I've seen people arrive at shows alone and I always felt sorry for them. How much fun would it be if you were there on your own—if no one cared whether you won or lost? Remember, this is just in my mind—it's not the truth about people who drive to shows on their own! I soon realized that I'd never *wanted* to drive the horse trailer, as it didn't conjure up any great images for me; it just wasn't part of how I saw myself. But at least I could now be honest about it!

Nearly every time you do an exercise like this, some strong identity issues will become evident. This is really important because we always (unless we make a conscious decision otherwise) tend to act consistently with our self-image. However, when we can examine our own issues more closely we can begin to question whether these things are consistent with who we are. For instance, I see myself as someone who would help others who were in difficulty, but supposing somebody needed my help and I couldn't give it because I couldn't drive the horse trailer? I also see myself as a very practical person, and I pride myself that my books aren't simply theories but they genuinely work— I had to get out there and prove it! So in the end I made the decision to drive the horse trailer because, as

"Doesn't-Suffer-Fools-Gladly Lady" pointed out, I am quite capable of doing so. And she was right!

Please note, though, that after doing this exercise I did not jump into the truck and trailer and take it for a spin up the highway at 70 mph. I realized (because I've taken on board the advice of the other chapters in this book) that it was first necessary to learn to drive the horse trailer safely. So, take my advice on this one—have some lessons with an experienced driver, learn the different rules for trailers and start off on easy roads without horses on board.

As part of my journey towards change I also explored all the reasons why I really am willing to drive the trailer. I wrote out another list and then, using mental imagery, felt how wonderful it was going to be when I was back behind the wheel:

I am now willing to drive the horse trailer because if there's ever an emergency I will be able to come to the rescue and save the day.

I am now willing to drive the horse trailer because people will be really impressed and say. "My goodness, aren't you amazing being able to drive that great big horse trailer?" (Our imaginations always love a bit of exaggeration!)

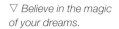

▽ *Believe in the magic of your dreams.*

YOUR turn to take the wheel (so to speak)

Now it's your turn. Isn't it exciting? This is going to be life-changing!

Start now. Write down, "I am now willing…", then your goal and then, "Why I am not willing" and your reason for this. When you've completely exhausted your supply of reasons, take a break and then go back and examine them to see whether some really are not valid and whether other reasons now come up for you. At the very end of all this, write an inspiring list of all the advantages you can enjoy by being able to do your new activity. That is the list to read through every day!

Of course, everyone's unique, but in all sorts of different circumstances the following objections are popular; look at how you might start answering the objections yourself.

"If I become confident and successful, people won't like me as much."
Sadly, this could be true: it is a fact that even people who love you don't always want you to change, even if (or, more particularly when) it's for the better. Such change alters the hierarchy of your relationship with them and, most disturbingly, it can make people feel that *they* should make changes (not always a comfortable feeling, as you know!).

So just be honest. How would you feel if your best friend made some changes and qualified her horse (whom she bought for $1,000) for the Rolex Three-Day Event or the Maclay Finals? Or if your mother suddenly started a new career and is now jetting round the world with celebrities? Yes, I know, you'd be pleased for them, but might you feel just the tiniest bit, ermm, unsettled?

Perhaps you do need to make a choice between being popular or successful; but there are people out there who are both successful and popular, aren't there? And maybe your true friends will learn to accept the new and improved you. If not, then they probably weren't great friends to start with.

"Moms don't win events. They don't gallop and they don't jump."
Oops, someone forgot to tell Olympic medal and Badminton winner Mary King about that. Imagine what a great role model you'd be as a successful, bold rider.

"If I didn't feel frightened I wouldn't have any excuse for not achieving."
Well, yes, that's true, but you don't want to be mediocre, do you? We know you're on the road to better things or you wouldn't have picked up this book!

"My friends are very supportive and I would miss that if I didn't need it any more."
Here's something radical: ask your friends to be supportive even if you don't look like you need it. Ask them if they would mind saying, "Well done, you, that was great," even if you found it easy. And if after a while you find you don't need that validation? That's OK; they can stop doing it!

"If I say I'm not good at something or am too nervous to try and people persuade me into it, then if it doesn't work they're partly responsible. So it's not really my fault. If I just leap in and try, people will think I'm arrogant and not support me if it doesn't work."
It's possible to manage people's expectations by saying, "I'm willing to try and see how I do." You don't have to always predict that you'll do it badly!

You should now be getting the idea, and you know that you can refute these statements.

Many things are revealed when you start being absolutely honest with yourself. However, it's a difficult process to go through; some people habitually lie to others by saying things like, "I'm so sorry I was late; it was the traffic" (you didn't know roads have other cars on them? Or was it that you left the house 20 minutes late, and wouldn't have got there even if the roads had been completely clear?), but we lie to ourselves even more.

Is the real issue that you need more motivation?

Think about this one; for instance, I "lack confidence" in my cooking because my sister and mother are much better at it than me and if I try to cook when they're around they say, "Look, it's really better if you just concentrate on the horse career, we'll do this." (And they've got a story about me burning some sausages in 1986.) I've also always had boyfriends who cook or take me out to dinner and, to be perfectly honest, this is all fine by me! However, if George Clooney was coming round and I heard that he wanted a woman who could cook—well, give me time, but I'd go out and get the best Cordon Bleu cookery lessons. I'd visualize, I'd practice, I'd deep-breathe—I'd find a way to do it, somehow (please don't tell George—he might think I'm too obsessive).

So how does this relate to people and their riding? Presumably you watch people jump round the Grand National? (Well, maybe.) Do you imagine they are not frightened? I jumped some of the Grand National fences for the film *Champions*. I'd never jumped "fences" before, although I had showjumped and been hurdle-racing. As soon as I had the offer for the film I was so excited to tackle those fences, but at the same time I honestly thought, "I've got a good chance of being killed here." But I so wanted to do it that I got on an old horse that someone lent me, and we just jumped those fences (bless him).

You see, sometimes it's purely about motivation: if you want something enough, you do it. If I said, "If you do this thing you claim you'd really like to do but lack confidence to do, I'll give you a million dollars for your favorite charity/this will save hundreds of ponies lives/(you fill it in…)."—if this was the case, do you think you could now do this thing you say you can't?

Supposing those offers don't work for you, but someone you hate says to you, "You'll never be able to do anything because your horse is an ugly old donkey." Could that be the incentive you need?

If your answer is, "Yes, of course I'll jump round the local show for a good enough reason," then at least we're quite clear that it's not fear that's the problem but motivation; and so motivation is the thing we'll start to work on.

So, now it's make-your-mind-up time—do you honestly want this or not?

No more excuses.

Do you expect never to feel fear, so that when you do it seems a message to be heeded?

A lot of this book is about how to feel more confident and how to lose those niggling fears and doubts. However, to expect never to feel fear is a bit unrealistic. As I've said before, you have to do a sensible risk analysis, but once you've determined that the risks are acceptable, you may just have to get on with it.

Public speaking is often cited as the number-one fear, with death a close second. This means that many people would rather be in the coffin at a funeral than delivering the eulogy. Unless you're the prime minister,

CASE STUDY

Susan Swann – not even good enough for lessons

I have even in the past not booked lessons because I felt I wasn't good enough to have them. Now, how silly is that? It took my daughter, who is 30 years younger than me, to put that into perspective. She said, "You have lessons to improve, not to show off how well you can do. No matter what level of ability you have—book the lesson!" I have since been working with one of Kelly's Intelligent Horsemanship Recommended Associates, Julia Fisher, and she's wonderful. She's made it clear: "We're not looking for perfect, we're just looking for better."

"He's no threat"

One of my niece Daisy's ambitions was to qualify for the Horse of the Year Show in the Working Hunter of the Year class. Daisy and Pie's relationship had not been without some problems, coupled with the fact that Pie is not what you'd call a typical show horse and is even a little bit small for his class. So when we arrived at Kent County Show for the qualifier we weren't what you might call "overconfident."

When Daisy rode round the collecting ring she heard two of the most successful riders talking about who might qualify, then she heard one say, "American Pie is here, but *he's* no threat." But she didn't let it get her down, quite the opposite. Pie didn't let it get him down either. Although he couldn't improve his conformation mark, he got the exceptional score of 10 out of 10 for manners and 20 out of 20 for style when jumping, and he went on to win the class and qualify for the Horse of the Year Show.

Becoming half the woman I was, for my horse

I have owned my pony for 3 years in August. He means the world to me: I worship the ground he walks on and, to be honest, he saved my life, because I was suicidal with depression before I bought him.

However, I have never ridden him. Reason? Too heavy, much too heavy. All I want to do is ride him. Nothing serious, just to potter about the farm and maybe some pleasure rides. So this year, I have lost nearly half my body weight—just for him. Yes, it's lovely to be able to wear nice clothes and feel healthy/look better, but the real reason I have been able to do it is him!

I have been advised that he can carry 125 pounds, as he has an old back injury and slightly arthritic hocks. I have 9 more pounds to lose… So, within the next few weeks I will be riding him for the first time ever! I am so very excited, it's all I think of night and day. But then we have another hurdle to overcome, and that is my nerves!

I'm the kind of rider that sometimes wants to throw up. Old accidents and memories—that sort of thing. My pony is also half Arab, and while he is a brave boy and likes to take charge and look after you, he does have a snort and huff at strange things. Not ideal for me, really, but the love I have for him is so great that now I want to overcome that as well (once I've tackled my weight), so that we can share a wonderful partnership for the rest of our time together.

FENELLA MAXWELL

there are virtually no physical risks attached to public speaking (but then even the prime minister shouldn't be unduly worried, with all the security surrounding him). Yet you may feel very frightened when you give your first talk: not just excited, but actually afraid. So does this mean you shouldn't go ahead? I don't think so, it just means that you need to practice the deep breathing and visualization exercises from chapter 4.

Recognize that this is the first step on your journey to becoming a confident public speaker. Be aware that if you continue to give talks, the time will come when speaking in front of large groups of people will barely cause a flutter, and you'll look back on your knee-quaking days and smile with wry amusement.

It isn't any different for *them;* they just get on with it

Fred Winter was four times champion jump jockey during the 1950s, and was often referred to as "Mr. Grand National"—because he'd ridden the winner of the Grand National twice, as well as many, many other victories. This man was brave, really brave: many would say fearless.

Fred also used to ride a horse called Mandarin, who not only won the Hennessy Gold Cup and the Cheltenham Gold Cup, but entered folklore after his final victory at the notorious Grand Steeplechase de Paris in June of the same year, 1962. At the third fence, the rubber bit in Mandarin's mouth broke and Fred was left with three and a half miles of a complex, and frighteningly difficult, course to negotiate with only his legs and the weight of his body to steer the horse. The story goes that the French jockeys rallied to the cause and used their mounts to help guide Mandarin round the bends. However, despite everything, Mandarin hung on to win by a head and was immediately retired. Fred finished riding two years later, having ridden a record 923 winners, before he went on to become a highly successful trainer.

Fred used to play golf with my father on a regular basis in their later years. Dad had such respect for him that he could never quite bring himself to call him "Fred" but, like many people, he called him "The Guvnor." Once, when they were talking about their riding days, Dad, who has ridden a fair few winners over jumps himself, confessed to Fred he really felt sick with worry before the jump races and only did it because he needed the

△ *"Courage is not the absence of fear, but rather the judgement that something else is more important than fear."* Ambrose Redmoon

money. Fred, who could be a bit gruff at times, surprised Dad by saying, "So how do you think I felt then, you bloody idiot?" Dad was amazed. "So why did you keep on going so long?" he asked. "Well, the problem was," Fred paused, "I just kept riding winners…"

Fear of failure: "You can't win unless you're prepared to lose"

Now I'm not saying you shouldn't hate failing with a *passion*, after all, if you don't care then you're losing one of your prime motivators—albeit a negative one.

Some people are driven to success in business, for instance, not by wanting to be rich, but by not wanting to be poor. We're all wired in different ways and whether it's carrot or stick that motivates you, as long as you *are* motivated in some way then the chances are you are going to achieve what you set out to do. The problem comes if you're the sort of person who is so frightened of failure they don't even try—that will really work against you.

It was my father who taught me about having to be "willing to lose" when I was riding in races. If you're riding on a circular racecourse it's pretty obvious that the shortest route is around the inside, however, some people are never willing to go around the inside because they're fearful of getting "boxed in" (meaning that they wouldn't be able to get through the other horses and therefore won't be able to win). Instead they play it safe and go right round the outside, making their horse run a much greater distance than the others. And then they lose anyway.

Just as with riders, I've never met or heard of a single successful person who hasn't "failed" somewhere along the line. Of course you don't want to fail, but you also need to be smart enough to know that failing is an important part of the winning process: it's what you have to do to achieve success.

Sometimes it's the most talented people who are heavily knocked by a setback and as a result you never hear of them again. These people are not used to having to take stock and then find the determination to put in the extra effort. That's good, though, because it gives the rest of us a chance! You and I are the ones who find that our disappointment will fire us up with determination to get things right the next time.

People who can't tolerate some frustration and give up on things too easily will never gain the depth of experience necessary to really know an area. It's not just the depth of knowledge that you gain by persisting with things, it's also the amount of confidence you gain by knowing that you CAN succeed if you put your mind to it.

One of the main organizers in the Intelligent Horsemanship office is Gitte Monahan. In the four years that Gitte (pronounced "Gidda"—it's Danish) has been here she's been incredible about taking over really complicated tasks and making them work. She's taken responsibility for many of "my" jobs, such as organizing the demonstrations and corporate days, so that I have more time to write and teach (and sleep!). She's good with horses as well as people and she teaches on the courses part-time too, which she really enjoys. It was strange, though, because at one time this looked like it was never going to happen. I'll let Gitte tell her own story…

Addressing the fear, and deciding that failure is better than nothing

When Kelly said that I could start doing some teaching on the courses it sounded an exciting prospect, but in order to do this I would first need to take the Stage 2 exams for the Monty Roberts Preliminary Certificate of Horsemanship (MRPCH), which meant facing my fears…

The thought of doing anything remotely "academic" was not something I wanted to entertain because it triggered memories that I wanted to keep buried—school and learning did not hold pleasant associations for me. The fear of getting it wrong, and the humiliation I was put through, made me freeze to the point of not being able to think.

Despite the negative environment of bullying, aggression and fear, I had always tried hard at school, but one particular incident led me to feel differently. I was deliberately ignored in class by a teacher when asking for help, and the despair of having my efforts thwarted yet again finally extinguished my enthusiasm to keep trying.

So how did I overcome the negative thoughts of the past? I wanted to succeed in my goal to progress with horses and teaching and it was Kelly who gave me some instrumental advice; she said, "You have to be prepared to fail," and that it didn't matter if I failed an exam because it could be re-taken the next year. This attitude was both scary but liberating at the same time, as although it meant I'd have to put myself in the vulnerable position that I might fail, the fact that there was no judgement on the outcome relieved any pressure and fear of *not* succeeding. Knowing this helped me to study for the exams in a far more relaxed frame of mind.

My renewed learning was greatly helped by the support of family and friends, particularly from my friend Rosie who was also taking the exams, as she gave me so much inspiration by her confidence and enthusiasm.

I am delighted to have passed the exams and proud to have gained the MRPCH which has enabled me to further develop my work with horses. This positive experience has changed my attitude towards learning, and it has also given me a sense of humility. Sometimes you have to put yourself in situations that you are uncomfortable with or that are challenging, as these are often the times that you learn the most and are the most rewarding.

Working with horses has highlighted to me how important "the teacher's" job is; there is a lot of responsibility and the actions of the trainer can have a long-term effect on the horse, good or bad. So as I have now learned, a good trainer can make all the difference!

GITTE MONAHAN

"It's got to be-e-e-e-e-e perfect!"

Closely linked to a fear of failure is the desire for everything to be perfect all the time. Sometimes knowing that you might not be able to attain perfection can hold you back from even trying.

I recently heard an interesting interview with a "perfectionist." The interviewer asked, "How do you know when something isn't perfect?" To which the perfectionist replied, "Because I notice all the things that are wrong." Next question: "So is this what you focus on?" The answer, "Yes, I tinker around with it endlessly, trying to get it right." "Do you ever get there; is it ever right?" "Well, no, it's never perfect." "So, what you really are is an 'imperfectionist,' focusing on everything that's wrong, and never reaching 'perfect'?"

Be your own person

If you need people to think well of you every hour of every day, then you'd better live alone and only look outside for your home deliveries. Even then you might find someone peering through your window laughing with others about how you just lie on your sofa all day. So, embarrassed about what other people think? You've got to get over yourself!

Sometimes I decide to go for a walk and I think it would be good for Pie to come out with me too (sadly, I don't have a dog at the moment), so I take him with me. It makes perfect sense to me—we both get some exercise. (Plus, of course, conversation feels more intimate when your heads are level—Pie's a very good listener.) It might seem strange to people who see me—a grown-up woman leading a funny little pinto horse around. Especially as I live in Lambourn—the "Village of Racing." But why should I be restricted in doing something that keeps me happy and fit and also keeps Pie happy and fit? Of course, if people came out and started stoning us then I might have to think again, but generally people just smile and nod.

Perhaps I'm just lucky to live in Britain, where a little bit of eccentricity is tolerated—and perhaps even secretly admired?

Time to live, not exist

A work colleague once said to me, "Gill, when you die, your tombstone will read: 'She wished she'd done x, y and z,' and on mine it will say, 'I bet you wish you hadn't done x, y and z!'"
I was at a point in my life where I couldn't cope with any type of failure or rejection, and my colleague was was right to say this because it spurred me on. I was existing, not living, and it took a rather tongue-in-cheek comment to make me decide to grab life.

Now when I'm nervous, I remember that none of us knows what's around the corner, so I try to focus on living every day and enjoying every minute. I look at my mom who saved and worked hard all her life and at the age of 58 developed cancer. She has been fighting it for 7 years now, in different parts of her body. All that going without to save for the future has meant she didn't do much of what she dreamt of, and it's heartbreaking to see her regret what she's missed. It's really made me re-evaluate what I need to do now, for me—hence my decision to attend an Intelligent Horsemanship course. I couldn't afford to, really, but I needed to do it for myself because it was always an ambition of mine.

Recently I went to see my doctor and I'm awaiting further tests, praying I'm not going to join my mom in fighting a hereditary illness. But for now I'm riding and doing all the things that I won't allow worry to keep me from. Maybe confidence is about trusting in a future of happiness and allowing dreams to become a reality—not allowing self-doubt to become reality.

I had to do my jumping assessment last week and having had a fall the last time I jumped (and not being able to ride for four weeks because of it), I was very nervous. So I focused on how proud I would be of myself if I gave it a try and how regretful I would be if I chickened out. I did one canter around and a practice over the first jump, and then went for it. I concentrated on the horse, getting him straight for the jumps, keeping him balanced and getting him on the correct leg—and although the round wasn't perfect, I passed the test.

I'm still very reserved, but now on my tombstone I would like a copy of that quote from *Become Perfect Partners*: "Life shouldn't be a journey to the grave with the intention of arriving safely in an attractive and well preserved body, rather gallop up, skid to a halt with chocolate in one hand, wine in the other, body thoroughly used up and totally worn out and screaming, WOO HOO... WHAT A RIDE!"

GILLIAN COLCHESTER

Identifying the enemy assignment

*"And I looked and I saw the enemy.
And the enemy was me."*

I am one of those people who find it useful to approach any challenge as a battle – dragon-slaying, if you will. This is great; as long as you have picked the right dragon!

The first step towards progress is to identify what needs changing, to know exactly what you're up against and what you can do about it.

Here's an exercise to help you make a positive plan for success:

First of all, choose a problem. By that I mean something specific, something that did or didn't happen that you aren't happy with. E.g., falling off, not getting on, not winning at showjumping or losing your temper.

Now you need to find as many reasons as you can to explain why you faced that problem.

BEWARE: Try not to come up with excuses instead of reasons. You can tell a reason from an excuse because a reason starts with, "I didn't" or "I haven't," whereas excuses tend to be in the past tense, and involve something that you did or didn't do (yet). You can convert an excuse into a reason pretty easily:

Why didn't I go to any shows last year?
EXCUSE: I didn't have any money. No one would drive the trailer.

Now ask yourself, "What could I have done to change this?" and, hey presto, your answer will have converted your excuse into a reason.

REASONS: I didn't prioritize enough money/earn enough money. I didn't learn to drive the trailer. I didn't organize anybody else to drive the trailer.

The next step in the exercise is to convert the reasons into plans for progress.

Sometimes this can be pretty obvious, such as:

PLANS: Learn to drive the trailer. Muck out for a friend in return for extra money for competing. Give up smoking to pay for competing, put an ad in a local paper for someone to drive the trailer, save up for a transport company, meet new hunky trailer-driving boyfriend, etc.

This is the great thing about this game: the more reasons you can come up with, the more plans for progress you can make. So don't be afraid to dive right in and spot your own weaknesses and mistakes. Admit your failings and celebrate your downfalls—in this exercise, the more ways in which you failed the more hope you have for future success!

Before you start, do make sure that the problem is actually a problem! For instance, if one of your reasons is, "I didn't want to," then you're either going to need to work on motivation issues and explore that aspect of the problem in more depth, or accept that it simply isn't something you're bothered about doing. Or perhaps you only think you *should* have competed last year because your friends think you should have?

So by identifying the "enemy" specifically, we are able to tackle the heart of the problem and approach the situation in a much more positive way. That cannot happen until you take responsibility for something you personally did or didn't do. Maybe it really was someone else's fault, but remember, the more things you can take some responsibility for, the more things you can change—so do try to find something that you did that might have contributed to the failure, if at all possible! Perhaps the person you relied on for that lift let you down, but perhaps you knew they were unreliable, or needed several reminders in the weeks before the event.

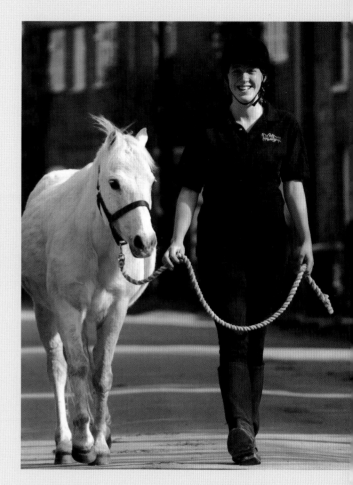

Rosie with organization issues, not Disorganized Rosie

If you find through these games that a specific personality trait, phobia or weakness is cropping up repeatedly in your reasons for past failures, then one of your plans for success is going to have to be tackling that weakness.

My own weakness is being disorganized. It crops up again and again when I go through the earlier exercise, and I can always come up with something specific to stop each particular problem recurring, but if I could learn to be more organized then I think many of my problems would be solved before they arise.

If an animal injures a limb he holds it close to him, and if a person has a weakness, she tends to do the same—defending her weakness and therefore protecting it. I'm sure you can all think of times when you have tried to help people and have been snapped at for your concern, or perhaps you have defended your own faults when others have tried to help. I myself have been guilty of this – I recall the number of times I told my mother (and myself) that I liked my room that way, and that it wasn't my fault I was disorganized.

I remember feeling wounded as if someone had insulted me personally when they were trying to tackle my problem with me. This defense mechanism is caused because we all feel vulnerable when we approach our weakest elements, but in defending ourselves against this feeling we are convincing ourselves that we don't want, or need, to change; thus making progress impossible.

In my case I had got in a muddle over who the enemy and the allies were. Because I saw disorganization as a part of me, anybody trying to defeat it becomes an enemy. In actual fact, by disowning my organization issues it became obvious that my mother was the ally and the disorganization itself was the enemy. We need to strive to be more like those heroic people who find the strength and courage to amputate their own body parts in order to be able to survive a life-threatening situation. Gruesome, difficult, but their only path for success and survival!

To make it possible for you to rid yourself of your vice or weakness, you first need to make sure you can separate it from yourself; that way attacking it will feel less like suicide. For instance, don't look at yourself as a shy person, because that would mean that every time you address the shyness problem you are insulting yourself and so your natural defense mechanisms will prevent you from changing. Instead, look at yourself as a lovely, confident person who is overcoming a shyness issue.

Whatever your personal flaw, you need to become detached from it and begin to accept yourself without it before you can expect any change. Become the thin person with an eating problem, a brave person who is working on confidence issues, become Sharon who is improving her motivation, rather than Lazy Sharon. If you let your problem become part of your identity, you will never be able to get rid of it.

So start now, redefine yourself as someone you want to be, identify your new enemies and you can start plotting ways to beat them.

Incidentally, I came to this way of thinking through working with difficult horses. I needed to find a way that I could still love a horse who had just tried to kill me, and separating the horse from his behavioral problem seemed to be the way to do it. Thinking this way makes it much harder to take it personally when you are being chased out of the field, and it enables you to love him but also fix his problem. In the same way, you need to respect yourself and disown your weakness.

ROSIE JONES, INTELLIGENT HORSEMANSHIP
RECOMMENDED ASSOCIATE

Checklist

- Have you done your "letting go" exercise?
- You say you want to do this or that, but are you really serious? What motivation would make you unstoppable in your efforts?
- Are you prepared to feel fear but still get on with things?
- Are you prepared to lose in order that one day you may win?
- Are you prepared to be less than perfect?
- Have you identified the enemies within you?

△ *Keep making time to appreciate the good things because it draws more good thing to you.*

CHAPTER EIGHT

Let's make it happen

TURN THOSE DREAMS INTO REALITY

Why you need to keep planting bulbs

As any gardener knows, if you want flowers to come up in spring you've got to plant your bulbs in autumn. This is not just advice for gardeners; it's a law of nature that we need to keep in mind all the time. Now, don't sit there thinking, "Why is she talking about planting bulbs? I want to fulfil my dreams and be confident with everything I do with my horse, right *now*!" But what we need to do is to start "planting our bulbs" right at this moment so that in 6 months' time we'll see real results. This is what will boost our confidence and encourage us to carry on to achieve our dreams, even if success with the big ones might be some years away.

If you're a performing seal you'll get rewarded with a fish for nearly every trick, and all good photographers know that models love them to say, "Wonderful, fabulous, stupendous, darling," with every click. A small child might need to get their reward for good work at least by the end of the day; others may work for a monthly allowance. The people who get (and deserve) the really big rewards, though, are those who are willing to work for months,

Whatever you can do—begin it. Boldness has genius, power and magic in it. Begin it now.

JOHANN WOLFGANG VAN GOETHE

even years, before they reap the benefits of their project. Have you ever heard the saying that it takes 10 years to be an overnight success? You and I, of course, really are planting our bulbs right now. I'm writing this book and working away with no reward or feedback. In a month or so it will all be finished and then that will be it. Nothing. I'll forget all about it and then suddenly "out of nowhere" the published book will arrive on my doorstep in September and anyone around at the time might think, "Well, how easy was that?"

You are planting your bulbs by reading this book and making plans for what you would like to happen in 6 months' time. Here, in the deepest winter of Lambourn, it would be easy to get depressed. I haven't even got a proper horse any more—I've just got this ball of mud who was Previously-Known-as-Pie. However, I'm planting my bulbs: I'm making sure he's well cared for (even if he does get a little dirty) and we're starting a gentle exercise program after his winter rest. If I don't put the work in now, I'm not going to have this cute little shiny skewbald to have fun with in the Easter holidays. That will be the real Pie—my beautiful little daffodil!

Write it down and make it happen

Putting your goals in writing is an extraordinarily powerful tool. Your mind is a goal-seeking mechanism, and if you help it out by being quite clear about what you specifically desire, then the subconscious mind will work day and night for you to help you achieve the results.

I have found that one of the most amazing things about goal setting is that there are times that I have written things down (my desires, dreams and wishes) and *forgotten all about the list* and then, some time later, I've found it in some old diary or the back of the drawer and realized that something I had written has actually come true. And without me "working on it" at all. I don't think that's how it's meant to happen, but it just goes to show the power of writing things down. It seems that just showing your amazing brain exactly what you want to achieve is enough for it to help you to do so, even without you being fully aware that you are doing it.

It is generally agreed, amongst those who recommend this approach, that when setting goals you should be as specific as possible. I, too, would advise that this is a good way to start, although be aware that sometimes

The best time to plant a tree was 40 years ago.
The next best time is today.

a higher power or your unconscious mind that draws things to you gives you even better alternatives than you could have imagined. It's very important, though, that when you write down a desired goal you should write it down *as if you have already achieved it*. For instance, you don't write, "I wish I owned a bright bay Connemara, who is very well behaved and good in traffic," but instead you put, "I *own* a bright bay Connemara, who is very well behaved and good in traffic."

So, the time has come. Remember those dreams you wrote about in chapter 3? Well, now is the time to start turning them into reality. Do you have your preliminary list ready? If so, now is a good time to sort through it and weed out any dreams that just don't inspire you any more. If you really can't imagine a particular goal being achievable and feel it just seems too far out of reach, then make a "stepping stone" goal with which you can be comfortable. For instance, if you have written down, "My horse wins the division championships," change it to, "My horse qualifies for the division championships." You get the idea. You've got to use a fair bit of imagination here, because I can't possibly know all your different ambitions!

The main goals

Personally, I think about 12 goals are enough to get you started—it's better not to overwhelm yourself at the start. Commit yourself to the following procedure for 6 months, during which time it is very important to note the little signs that "things are happening"—that phone call out of the blue, that "coincidental" meeting with just the right person. Be aware that these happenings often take the form of strange coincidences (called syncronicity, meaning "meaningful coincidence"). Every time you note one, appreciate it and gain confidence from realizing that you are now on the right track.

It's best if your goals support each other so, if your goal is to own a fabulous jumper, you might like to imagine how much you need to earn, or how you would find a sponsor, so you don't end up with a fabulous jumper in your garden shed, then set these up as the goals you are aiming for. You should also think about the personal qualities you're going to need to live the life you dream about, such as, "I am very disciplined and have high levels of energy."

Goal setting—what you do next

As you wake up, read through your list and take about 5 minutes to focus on the different things you'd like to achieve. Use every one of your senses to feel yourself being the person you want to be, and achieving the things you want to achieve. If any negative feelings or doubts crop up, don't fight them, just gently push them away and focus on the positive. Treat the insignificant little dream stealers as they deserve to be treated.

Before you go to sleep, read your list again and go through the same procedure and acknowledge any signs that things are working. If ideas pop into your head about someone you should get in touch with, or an idea that's relevant to your goal, make sure you act on it. If you start to feel less

ASSIGNMENT
Goal setting

To start you off, here is an example of 6 goals (2 in each category) to give you an idea of what you should be doing. Once you've read it through, it's your turn!

Material things: I own a beautiful safe horse, 7 years old, who is easy to handle in every way. (You can fill in more detail.)

I can afford to go on a wonderful safari holiday with my friends and ride with giraffes.

Personal qualities: I am full of energy and work hard on the things that matter, so I can achieve all my goals.

I have a really good relationship with all the significant people in my life. In fact, I make friends easily everywhere I go because I have an outgoing, generous personality.

Supporting factors: I'm lucky because my boss understands how important riding is to me and allows me flexible time off for important events.

I have passed my Intelligent Horsemanship foundation course so I feel more confident in my knowledge of horses.

enthusiastic about a goal it's perfectly all right to change it; in fact, do rewrite your list as often as you'd like.

During the day, if there is any possibility of taking a 10-minute complete relaxation break, then grab it! My osteopath advised me to lie down on the floor for 10 minutes every day with my head on the telephone directory to stretch my back out. Let's face it, most horse people have aching backs. This "meditative" time is the ideal opportunity for your subconscious mind to work on one of your personality goals and help you become the person you'd like to be—confident, brave, strong, whatever you feel is most appropriate.

Be aware too that sometimes a higher power has something better in mind for you than you ever imagined. When I first started setting myself goals the career I now have and love didn't even exist so, unsurprisingly, it wasn't on my list!

▽ At 51, Badger is the oldest horse in Britain. "Age does not protect you from love, but love to some extent protects you from age." Jeanne Moreau

Practical action plans

It's great to put your higher power/subconscious to work, but taking some positive action will be a great help too. In order to buy the right horse you need to learn all you can about it, including going to horse shows and asking people with the type of horses you like where they bought that horse and if there is a horse for sale. Keep putting out "feelers" and learn all you can about the subject you are interested in.

Maybe you feel it's hopeless because you think you could never afford to buy your own horse; you can only afford a riding lesson once a month. But you always have choices. You could sacrifice even that one lesson a month, take overtime at work and save every penny you earn so that you have the money you need in your bank account in 3 years' time. Or, if you're in a low-paying job anyway, perhaps you should go and work in a stable where you can be around horses and gain some additional qualifications. Start thinking about your action plan with the sure knowledge that there IS an answer out there and, sure enough, you'll find it. Feel free to write to me and tell me your answer when you find it!

"I can do anything but I can't do everything."

This saying is very apt for me, and maybe it is for you too. There are times when many of us are distracted by so many thoughts that we can't concentrate on anything and end up achieving nothing worthwhile.

In keeping with the current times, I have that perennial problem of too much to do but not enough time to do it in. I love running my courses, I enjoy writing and find it really satisfying, I need to answer emails, I want to spend time with friends, I want to spend time with my horses and help other people with theirs, I like to sleep for a decent amount of time, I enjoy luxurious baths, I enjoy reading and watching *The Apprentice* or Sarah Beeny in *Property Ladder*. I've gone through every time-management technique I knew was available to me (I had "to do" lists on post-it notes stuck on every wall of the house). Then I read a book that, to me, contained a revolutionary concept: "If you have tried all the time-management techniques available and you still feel you can't get through everything you need to do, then there is only one answer—you have to give something up." Incredible! That had never crossed my mind before. I do hope Sarah Beeny won't be offended.

"Don't let your dreams get stolen"

Mr. Fowler paced back and forth at the head of the class, while we students waited with our pencils sharpened and our paper ready. A tall man with an erect bearing and an olive complexion, he always dressed immaculately.

"I want you to think about this very carefully," said Mr Fowler, waving his long, elegant hands. "It should be like painting a picture of your lives in the future, as if all your ambitions had been realized."

A voice piped up. "How much detail d'you want, Sir?"

"As much as possible. It should be a complete portrayal of what you envision for yourselves in the future." He turned to gaze at us calmly. "And my last instruction to you is perhaps the most important: this vision of the future that you're all about to paint should be a realistic one. I don't want to hear about some crazy, off-the-wall plan. I don't want to know about any Hollywood dreams either."

There was a smattering of laughter at this idea. We were in California, after all.

He finished by saying, "It should be a fair and accurate assessment of where I might expect to find you if I were to visit you in your mid-thirties. It's to be called 'My Goals in Life' and should be returned within 3 weeks."

I was in my last year of high school, and this was one of the first projects we were set to do. It was an easy start for me, because I knew exactly what I wanted to do in life. In fact, it was a continuation of a useful exercise I'd already been doing for myself over the years. I'd started doing drawings of stables and training facilities when I was 9 years old.

Given my subject matter, I didn't have to worry about Mr. Fowler's final instruction either, as mine was no Hollywood dream, even though I'd been in countless films by this time. So I pressed ahead with the assignment and I turned in what I thought was a good paper on the subject. It was the ground plan and associated paperwork for the running of a thoroughbred racehorse facility.

Five days later the paper was returned to me with a big red "F" printed across the top of the page. Also written were the traditional words: "See me."

This was a shock, because I was accustomed to achieving good grades. I went immediately to see Mr. Fowler after class, showed him my work again and asked what in the world I'd done wrong.

He leafed through the pages and said, "You know that my last instruction to you was to be realistic in this projection of your future?"

I replied, "Yes, I did realize that."

"Do you realize what the annual income of a person in the United States is?" he asked me.

I replied, "No, I'm sorry but I don't."

"Sixty-three hundred dollars!"

I waited for him to continue, but I had a clear idea of what he was going to say next.

"So how many years would you have to work and save up to earn the amount of money you'd need for your plan?" he asked me.

"I don't know."

He tapped his finger against the red "F" and advised me, "It is a wild, unattainable dream. That is why I gave it a failing grade based on the instructions that I issued at the outset." Then he handed back the paper. "I know your family and background; it would just not be possible. Take it home, think about it, change it to an appropriate level and hand it in again. The last thing I want is to fail you based on a misunderstanding."

It felt like he'd driven a knife into me—his reaction was that unexpected. I was suddenly awakened to the reality of finance and I faced the prospect that my dream could never be realized.

The next two or three days were depressing, I was at home agonizing over what to do. I couldn't figure out how I could change it. My mother saw I was in trouble and asked what was wrong, so I confided in her.

She read my paper and suggested, "Well, if that's truly your life's dream, then in my opinion you can achieve it. I think you ought to consider turning the paper back in just the way it is, without any changes." She added, "If you think it's unattainable, then you can change it yourself. But I don't think it's fair for a high school instructor to set a level on your hopes and dreams."

I recall feeling renewed at that point.

I returned to school and handed the paper back the same as before, except with an additional note written on it that his perception as my instructor that it was unattainable was fair enough, but my own was that it was attainable as a life plan, and that I didn't think he had a right to put a cap on my perceptions. He should grade the paper as he thought fit.

When the grades were mailed to us, I did get an "A" for that particular course. I never did find out to what extent he changed the mark, but I couldn't have achieved an "A"' overall if he'd left that paper with an "F" grade.

I didn't know it then, but I was to come into contact with Mr. Lyman Fowler much later in my life, in 1987 when the boot would be firmly on the other foot.

MONTY ROBERTS, FROM *THE MAN WHO LISTENED TO HORSES*

Is your life made of sand or rock?

A time-management expert was giving a lecture to a group of students. He stood in front of them with a table in front of him, and on that table stood a large glass cylinder. "This cylinder," he told the students, "represents your day, and I am going to start filling it with things." At this the expert took out three large stones and placed them, one on top of the other, in the glass cylinder.

"Is the cylinder full?"' he asked. "Yes!" answered one of the students. At which the teacher took out a bag of smaller stones and poured them into the glass cylinder. "Is the cylinder full now?" he smiled. The students were very bright and caught on quickly. "No," they called. The expert took out a bag of sand and proceeded to empty it into the cylinder. "What can we learn about time management from this exercise?" he enquired. One student put up his hand and answered, "No matter how busy you think you are, you can always add in something else." The expert smiled. "The lesson we learn from this is that if you want the big stones in, you have to put them in first. Your job is to decide what your big stones are and make sure they go in first."

I have certainly been guilty at times of thinking I can do everything, and this book (which I've wanted to write for some time) was never going to get written because of hundreds of outside distractions. Although many of these were enjoyable and fulfilling in their own right, I knew that if I really wanted to write the book then I had to make some decisions: I had to work out what I was able to fit into my life and what I wasn't. The question I had to ask myself was, "If writing the book is important, what do I have to give up in order to achieve it?" because, unless you have many unstructured hours just waiting to be filled in your day, then there's always a price to pay!

Of course, it's up to you to decide what's a fair price to pay and, of course, I knew that once I'd written the book (having made some sacrifices in other areas), I would be able to get back to the general "busyness." Or perhaps, after this project, I might make planning Pie's "Guest Appearance" in my next demonstrations the most important thing to me in the next 6 months, and that might mean I won't have time for other work or even time to browse in bookshops. Certainly we need balance in our lives, but to achieve that we have to be prepared to make choices.

I once watched an Oprah Winfrey "Change Your Life" TV show in which she interviewed a man who had lost some amazing amount of weight, something like 140 pounds, I think. He talked about how he had saved up some money and taken a year off work to fully concentrate on losing weight. I thought then, what a great idea, and how brave of him. The reason I say brave is because I think it's easy for all of us to make excuses, but excuses never get results. Making such a big commitment to his goal like that was a very public way of stating his intention. Not having other distractions in his life (like earning a living) meant that he could be sure he would be able to prepare healthy meals every day and never have to miss a workout because he was having to work late, or was just too tired when he got home.

So, how are we going to fit it all in? If we can't take a year off to concentrate on one thing—or indeed don't want to take the time off because we love our job—then what are we going to do?

Obviously I don't know all your circumstances—whether you have your own horse (maybe your goal is to own one) or you take riding lessons once a week and you'd just like to achieve a little more with your riding (i.e., not fall off at the trot/learn how to jump)? Or maybe you have your

Every single day I failed

Use what you've learnt with horses for yourself as well: break things down into easily achievable steps. I planned to write this book in some "time off," putting in 14-hour days of writing. That was never going to be realistic and so it meant that every day I failed. If every day you fail, then you end up feeling like a failure (not the best state to be in). I changed my daily "to do" list from, "Write book, answer every email, organize October tour and Pie and I get fit," to something like, "Write 1000 words, spend an hour on emails, make preliminary list of venues for October tour and ride Pie for 45 minutes," I got to know how success feels again, and things became easy and fun and I was able to achieve far more.

Don't forget: "If at first you do succeed—try not to look too surprised!"

Why not ask for help?

I work in London during the week and I treat each day (starting at 6:51am) on the train and the London Underground as an adventure. People cram on to the Underground with no room to move; if I tried to transport my horse in the same conditions I would/should be arrested. What occurred to me recently, though, was that just because we might tolerate inconveniences for work, that doesn't mean we should have to do the same for our "pleasure."

Over Christmas one of my directors proudly told me about his wife who, in her mid-forties, had always wanted a horse. So for Christmas he arranged a stall at a local barn and gave her a check for her to buy her ideal horse.

She was very thrilled, as you can imagine, and her horse was everything she wanted. So

she went about her duties with real commitment, insisting on doing everything herself—all the mucking out, cleaning, grooming and feeding. She was at the stables at 7:00 am every single day and then again to put her boy to bed, 7 days a week. Unfortunately, she just wore herself down and after a couple of years she decided that she could not give her lovely horse the time he needed and sold him. Another dream bites the dust, I thought.

The point of my story is that, however much we love our horse, our children or our dog, there is no disgrace in getting some help when we need it. Yes, and even allowing ourselves a few days off from time to time! As it happens, this lady could easily have afforded to have paid someone to help, and I don't know why she didn't feel she could choose that option. Perhaps not all of us are so fortunate to be able to pay someone to help us, but then why not set up a rotating system at your stables, where you help each other out and give each person one day a week off? While you're at it, you might think about having your neighbours' children over while they go shopping and vice versa— think how much happier the children will be for not having to go round the supermarket!

Would that be cheating, do you think? Why? Who makes these rules? Do we feel better for making it hard for ourselves? Do we think it makes us better people if we make life difficult?

SANDRA O'HALLORAN

own horse but there are a few problems—you'd like to get nearer to the perfect partnership? Maybe your goal is to be an Intelligent Horsemanship Recommended Associate one day? Or maybe your horse is going so well that you'd like to compete on him yourself, or find someone who would compete him at a show for you?

ASSIGNMENT
Dream book

Cut out pictures of the things you wish to own (like your ideal horse or barn) and pictures that represent the experiences you want to have (winning competitions, riding with friends, perfect job, being at your ideal weight, more peace or balance in your life), to remind yourself of how you want it to be. Tape them up where you will see them every day—on the mirror, the refrigerator, or your bulletin board.

Practical day-to-day goals

Let's imagine you really do want to ride in the Kelly Marks' Perfect Partners Winter Trec series. (I chose that particular competition because I like the name so much.) My event is based on the BHS TREC, which is a unique equestrian sport based on the French discipline, "Le Trec."

Introduced to England by the British Horse Society in 1998, BHS TREC appeals to a variety of riders with all kinds of horses and ponies. The competition is designed to test a horse/rider combination through a whole range of activities rather than focusing on one particular discipline. The sport requires versatility and training, combining the requirements of trail-riding with jumping and correct basic flatwork.

Budget Life Coach assignment

It's always easier to see the mistakes that other people are making, and much harder to see our own and how we might be working against our own best interests. So what I'd like you to do now is first to take a look at the goals you have written down, and then I want you to step out of your own body (metaphorically, of course) and examine your day-to-day (even hour-by-hour) actions, and say whether the actions of this person (i.e. you!) look like they are those of someone who is going to achieve the goals you have written down.

If you've written down (let's say), "My horse and I are going so well now we have won 3 competitive trail rides," then take a look at how you've been spending your time over the last month. See if your actions have indeed been those of someone who is likely to win 3 such competitions. As your own consultant, would you believe that "your client" was serious about their stated intentions? What would you advise they should do to be more likely to bring about the results they (say they) would like?

BHS TREC comprises three phases: testing the partnership's ability to cope with an all-day ride across varied terrain, route finding and negotiating natural obstacles and hazards, while also considering the welfare of the horse, respecting the countryside and enjoying all it has to offer. One of the best things about this competition for the less ambitious competitor is that you can leave out any of the obstacles or hazards if you wish and you won't be eliminated, but will just lose the number of points allocated to that obstacle.

I particularly like this event because it's one of the most friendly horse and rider competitions I know of, and nearly all the things that are going to help you do well in the competition will help you with your everyday handling and riding of your horse too.

Now you have a vague idea of the event, but for this exercise I'd like you to work hard to think things through. Do you have the rule book and have you read it thoroughly? Have you been to a Trec competition, purely to watch it and get a flavor of how it works and what to expect? How are you going to get there? Readers from the US will need to arrange airfare and a horse to ride. What is the dress code? It's a good idea to write down every area you need to consider then work out a plan from this list.

It's fun to use big pieces of paper, and lots of color for this sort of thing, but use whatever works for you. Brainstorm everything you think you might need to consider. What level of support and preparation do you think you might need?

Have you done your brainstorming? Good. Here are just a few considerations that occurred to me:

If you want to be able to load your horse, reliably, at different times of day, even if it's early in the morning:
The answer to this one is obvious—just do it again and again and at different times of day, when there are different activities going on around you. (If your horse is not already a good loader, there are plenty of ways in which Intelligent Horsemanship can give you help with this—so contact our office.)

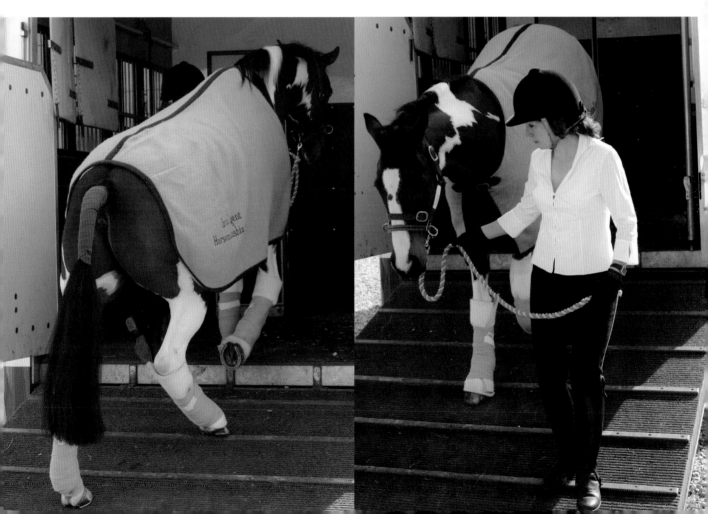

▽ *Can you get your horse into a horse trailer? And out calmly too?*

Get out more!

One of the best ways to put all of the points opposite into practice is to load up and take your horse somewhere new for a hack. Not only can this be a great way to explore those areas slightly further afield, but it is also invaluable initial preparation. Once your horse is happy doing this, you might want to take him to clinics or somewhere for lessons, which will be a little more like a show atmosphere. (If you can ride to the venue, all well and good, but you still need to make sure that your horse is prepared for the sort of route you will be taking.)

If you want to be able to unload your horse when you get to the show, or have him stand quietly in the trailer:
It's quite a big deal for a lot of horses to just stand in the trailer, so, again, practice this one. Initially, go for quite short periods of time and then gradually build it up.

If you want to be able to tie him up with a haynet while you get him ready:
It's best not to leave your horse unsupervised, but it is handy if he will stand quietly with someone "keeping an eye on him," as opposed to someone having to cling onto him for dear life while you go off to the restroom! The success of this might also depend on being able to recruit help.

If you want to load him up at the end of the event, even if there is still lots of excitement going on:

If competing in the winter, you might have to consider the possibility that it will be dark either when you are leaving home or when you are returning from the show. So making sure you have lights that work in the inside of your trailer will be very important.

◁ Will your horse stand by a trailer, relaxed?

If you want to get him to stand nicely to be tacked up:

It may be that you have to braid the horse's mane, too, or you might feel you want to. Obviously you will do that at home, but you might need to make some running repairs while out and about. You will probably need to do a bit of tidying after the journey so it's important he's able to settle when he's somewhere new.

If you want to stand nicely to be mounted:

Your horse might usually stand perfectly at home, but it's a bit less likely in a more exciting environment. Equally, it is extremely unlikely that if he fidgets at home he will suddenly stand still at a show (unless he is so

◁ As Daisy walks the course at the Royal Windsor Horse Show, I'm keeping Pie relaxed and calm for her.

surprised and distracted by all the activity that you are able to take advantage of one of his staring-into-space moments!). Again, taking him to unusual places may give you the opportunity to practice this, and it also helps if you feel well able to deal with your horse in more demanding situations.

Will my horse be safe once I'm on him in a new environment?
Most showgrounds have an area where you can double-line lunge your horse to settle him down. Two lines are much preferred to single-line lungeing because, for one thing, you have so much more control.

Are you experienced with your double-line lungeing? If not, read *Become Perfect Partners* and get some lessons from an Intelligent Horsemanship Recommended Associate.

Will my horse work well with others at a competition?
If you aren't sure whether this is the case, you will need to test it before you arrive at the showground. You can do this by having a trial run— where you pay to enter a competition but don't actually do the test. In this case you would probably also be allowed to enter the ring and ride around for a minute or two. (Obviously you could just turn up and "borrow" the show atmosphere, but it's more polite to pay a fee for this!)

Or you might find that riding clinics in which you share a lesson, or a group lesson, are good preparation. If your horse proves to be very territorial or is easily intimidated, you will need to address this before entering a competition. Some venues are much more crowded than others, but it is extremely unlikely that you will be able to get away with not taking your horse near others at all. Some venues don't allow stallions, and those that do won't expect to have to go to special lengths to accommodate them. You will need to make sure that a stallion can keep his mind on the job at hand (i.e., dressage!) even if there are sexy, in-season mares flirting with him.

Will my horse leave the others to enter the ring?
If you are traveling to the show with a friend, this could be a particular issue. Even if your horses aren't the best of friends at home, they can become unusually clingy in this situation. If the ring is in an indoor arena it is likely that the warming-up area will be outside (unless it is huge). If

you have any doubts about your horse's likely willingness to enter the arena, find out in advance if you are allowed help, then arrange for someone to assist you before the show, rather than calling out for help as the problem develops. This will help you to stay more confident.

Do my horse and I have the necessary fitness and ability to handle the obstacles in the competition?

Make sure that you are very comfortable with the movements, obstacles and hazards required of you. It is unlikely that your horse will suddenly be able to do something that he struggles with at home, in fact, quite the opposite. There is a rule of thumb that says you should compete at the level at which you were riding 6 months ago at home. This really becomes relevant when you are adding in more movements later on (lateral work and such), but it is interesting to note that this sort of drop-off in performance is pretty much expected. This leads me to the next point…

▽ *Gitte Monahan riding Folly and proving their ability and fitness in handling the obstacles.*

▷ Perfect preparation will help you keep things together when under stress.

Will we be able to hold things together under the stress?

It might be extremely useful to take some performance coaching sessions before a competition, which can maximize your chances of riding to the best of your ability. Even if nerves aren't an issue for you, performing at your best is usually more than a matter of gritting your teeth and going for it. In fact, gritting your teeth is unlikely to help! You may also find that these sessions help you get the most from your other riding sessions and lessons, and so could be well worth the investment.

The above are just the very basic points that occurred to me—but feel free to add more and write out your own complete list.

Checklist

- Which bulbs have you planted? (i.e., what great thing is going to happen in 6 months' time?)
- Have you written down your goals?
- Are you following through the steps to make them happen? As you wake up? As you go to sleep? During the day?
- Have you the time to do all the things you want to do? If not, have you decided what you must give up in order to have the time needed to achieve your most important goal?
- Have you made your daily goals achievable to you? Do you get a daily feeling of success?
- Are you finding a way to get help when you need it?
- Have you put together your Dream book?
- Have you started to put some concrete plans into action to achieve your goals? Would you be able to describe to me exactly what you've done? (Not what you're "going to do.")
- If you were looking at your life from the outside (i.e., as if you were your own life coach), how would you say you are doing?
- Have you thought of a goal and then written a complete list of the practical day-to-day things you need to achieve in order to reach your final goal?

CHAPTER NINE

To compete or not to compete?

AND THAT IS THE QUESTION

Competition, or at least "serious" competition, seems to be the dividing line between riders. Often people on my courses will define themselves by saying, "Oh, I don't compete or anything. I'm just a happy hacker." Or, "I do Intermediate 3-day eventing and I'm hoping to qualify for the next level soon." There are also a few people who fall somewhere in the middle, bashfully admitting to the odd Riding Club clear round, but the division in the horse world seems to be between those who "ride for fun" and those who "ride seriously" (often with quite a lot of prejudice on both sides about the "other" side).

For me, while there may be people who have developed extraordinary rapport and skills practicing alone with their horse, I find that going out into the "real" world—as in teaching, doing demonstrations, attending clinics or competing—is a fantastic way to learn. Working this way highlights one's weaknesses magnificently and, with the right attitude, can bring about a quantum leap in improvement.

◁ *Pie and Daisy taking first prize at Royal Windsor Horse Show.*

We act as though comfort and luxury were the chief requirements of life, when all that we need to make us happy is something to be enthusiastic about.

CHARLES KINGSLEY

▷ *Everyone remembers their first win.*

There are definitely pros and cons to competing, though, and if you're not interested in competition, that's fine (but keep reading just in case you change your mind). However, if competition is *the* reason you have for getting out of bed in the morning, that's great too. Remember the Nike ad? "Do it. Or don't do it." Why make it any more complicated than that?

If you decide that you would like to compete, then let me tell you it's an ideal way to bring focus into your training, to motivate you to ride even when the weather isn't perfect, to keep you on the ball as you learn the importance of "getting things right," and it gives you an excuse to spend hours fussing over the one you love (your horse, of course!). It also brings you lots of excuses to praise your horse (and they know when you're happy and proud of them), and also, if you are reasonably open and friendly, you get to meet other like-minded people who are passionate about spending time with horses. One other great advantage of competition is that, sooner or later, it teaches you that wonderful quality—*humility*. You don't understand what I mean? Ah, you've obviously never competed!

So what are you letting yourself in for?

It's as well to know the reality of competing before you start. There's a lot of work to be done if you start to take it seriously (when you could be watching television or having morning lie-ins instead); and it can also get very expensive (so say goodbye to those Gucci handbags and expensive dinners out).

There are people out there who think that their horses are there simply to make them look good and they never develop anything other than a very superficial relationship with their animals. Nearly as bad are the people who are good in competition and become very arrogant; who start thinking they are experts on everything and certainly have nothing more to learn about horses. There are also those for whom competing matters a very great deal; they often seem to lack perspective and behave very badly when things don't go their way. At the top level, too, there might be pressure (maybe from the sponsors) to compete the horse even if it's potentially detrimental to his health in the long run.

CASE STUDY

Sophie's first show

I can hardly remember my first show, but I can remember Sophie's. I had a 13.2hh pony, Holly, who was in for re-schooling, and after the initial work was done I needed a small jockey to continue her education. That was little Sophie—kind, sweet and with a halo of blonde curls.

Sophie had not competed before and was convinced she was not good enough to even ride around the showground, let alone compete. She only had borrowed show gear, and Holly wasn't a pretty, pointy-toes sort of pony. Sophie had preconceived images of Olympic-level riders passing snide comments at her and looking down on her and Holly.

The horses were pulled in to stand in the middle of the ring in any order, ready to do their individual shows. Holly's wild mane was at least partly restrained by hundreds of the wrong-colored plaiting bands and hair gel, her cheap tack had been cleaned impeccably and, overall, they looked pretty good (apart from Sophie's terrified expression!).

It was painful to watch Sophie at first, but then I saw something wonderful happen, and I realized that I had no need to be worried for her and that I too was guilty of underestimating "people at shows." What I saw was a slightly older girl on a beautiful pony smile at Sophie and ask, "What's your pony's name? She's lovely!"

Sophie's grimace melted into the most grateful smile. The two girls quietly chatted in the line-up, as the more experienced child gave Sophie a few good tips, then they wished each other luck. We came home with three ribbons, a very happy pony and some new friends! Sophie said to me on the way home, "I don't know why I was scared of the people at shows, after all, I am now a 'person who goes to shows' and I am nice!"

ROSIE JONES, INTELLIGENT HORSEMANSHIP RECOMMENDED ASSOCIATE

Many people have been put off competitions as children, having been exposed to win-at-all-costs parents at the shows and suspected corruption at the local pony club ("Did Mrs. Peregrine really invite the Hougton-Smythes to dinner just so Davina could win the best turn out?" "I certainly wouldn't put it past her!")

I'm not sure whether competition brings out the worst in people's characters, or whether it simply reveals it. Most of us can be nice when there's nothing at stake (although with some people, not even then). The good news is that these displays of negative character traits have more to do with the individual than with the act of competing itself, and you can simply choose not to be like that. If you go to a local event and stay open and friendly, there's every chance you'll meet a great many kind, generous, helpful people who just love being around horses.

Of course, people have different reasons for competing: for instance, for the professionals in racing and showjumping, amongst other disciplines, the reasons probably include making money. As in most industries, you need to be in the top 10 percent, otherwise you need an additional way to make a living. Even when money isn't a consideration, many people who consider themselves competitive, when asked why they compete, may well answer, "to win"—and yet is that really the case? If you merely want to win there's a guaranteed way to do so; you just make sure that you never, ever enter a competition where anybody in it might be better than you. Of course, there are a few "ribbon junkies" about but, for most people, taking a regular "A"-rated show winner to clean up at the local gymkhana would be somehow unfulfilling, if not downright embarrassing.

It's my belief that entering a competition is as much about enhancing our skills as measuring them. What can put people off, though, is that it's not always easy being under public scrutiny, because you are always at risk of being criticized—and who likes that? Perhaps you're the type of person who is very hard on themselves when you feel you haven't done as well as you should. But that's not all bad. Not being as successful as you think you should have been might make you feel uncomfortable, unhappy, annoyed or frustrated. You feel, "This is unfair," and then you think, "How can I do this better next time?" It is developing this attitude that is going to make you a winner in every area of your life.

Success in sports (particularly horse racing) can bring a certain amount of kudos amongst members of the public—especially those who bet on

you when you won (naturally enough, this is quickly reversed when you lose). The high point of my racing career was traveling in a London taxi when the driver said, "You're not Kelly Marks, are you? I backed you when you won on Tournament Leader at Salisbury—what a great race." Then he refused to take any money for my fare. Sadly, nothing else even approaching this has ever happened since; however, many times I sit in the back of taxis hinting, "Did you ever bet on horses before 1995?" "I used to ride in races, you know." The cabbies just turn up their radios or bring the subject back to politics and the weather.

△ *Riding Xylophone at Sandown. In racing, whether you are a hero or a zero can often depend on the length of your horse's nose.*

How to be a successful competitor

If you're a "serious competitor," your best way forward is to train with someone who is at the top of the profession in your chosen discipline. There are very few people who "make it" without experienced advice. Take every opportunity to study successful people, but remember that you only want to take the bits from their work that are appealing to you—if they are obnoxious and cruel they are most likely to be successful *in spite* of that, not because of it. You only need to study autobiographies in any area of expertise to find that there is usually a Merlin (King Arthur's magician) somewhere in the story. (See Finding a Mentor, chapter 6.)

Whether you're a "serious" or "just for fun" competitor, you need to realize that perfect preparation is the key to achieving the day of your dreams. Write out your checklists for all your arrangements, your clothing, your horse's tack, and leave absolutely *nothing* to the last minute. There is not to be one second of rushing around in a panic before the class. Due to lack of experience, there may be the odd thing you forget to consider at your first show, so if there is, make sure you write out a "things we'll do better next time" list and add it to your future checklists. Those people who have been competing all their lives have these details in their head, but when you're starting out you won't have this advantage, so you need to write things down.

If you go to a major show you'll notice that all the top riders arrive at least 2 hours in advance of the class, whereas if you go to a local show

▽ *Jumping off the bank at Hickstead.*

(note "local," meaning for people who live *near* the venue), you are bound to see several people at a time dash over to any given ring breathlessly asking, "Which class is this? Am I too late?" and if they're jumping, "Can anybody tell me what the course is?" You might not care about being "unprofessional," but what fun is it when you're unnecessarily stressed before you even start? Most importantly, it's not fair to your horse.

The power of rituals and routine

We've already discussed in chapter 8 the other checks we can make, but I'd like to remind you that you need to be performing the tasks you're going to do in the show really easily at home beforehand. If you and your horse can't perform easily when there's no pressure, it's unlikely that you'll be better when the pressure is on.

So get into a routine that enables you to work with minimum pressure. When Daisy was competing Pie they found a routine that worked for them:

"The less thinking people have to do the better," explains Walsh, the brilliant coach of the San Francisco 49ers. "When you're under pressure the mind can play tricks on you. The more primed and focused you remain, the smoother you deal with out-of-ordinary circumstances."

FROM *ON FORM* BY JIM LOEHR AND TONY SCHWARTZ

Daisy would arrive a couple of hours before the class, she would get Pie straight out to walk around the showground, then they'd look around and explore and do any socializing they chose to do. Then they'd come back into the horse trailer and Pie would have a small haynet while his braids were put in. Daisy would then eat some breakfast (brought along in the trailer), get changed into her show gear and they'd be ready 45 minutes before the class to walk down to the ring. If they weren't good enough on the day then they'd have to look at other areas for improvement, because it could never be down to being in a rush or being stressed.

Preparation for competition day

I'd like you to imagine now that you're going to a competition and you've written to me for advice on how you should best prepare for the actual day.

First of all you've made sure that you are playing to your strengths and that you've found the competition you and your horse are most suited to. By this time you should have practiced at home together extensively (it's

▽ "Before everything else, getting ready is the secret of success." Henry Ford

also essential to practice in different environments so you can see if you are able to carry the lessons with you anywhere), and ideally you will also have been to a few shows without competing (just to let your horse get used to the atmosphere and to see exactly what's required). You have been practicing when you're both calm and relaxed with no pressure, and you have been schooling near other horses, perhaps even been jumping a practice jump, if appropriate. You should have also purchased any necessary rule books and studied them, as being eliminated for something you should know about is very annoying. (Check through these carefully because there will probably be rules about not wearing jewelery, certain bits might be prohibited or the competition might have breed and open classes.)

Be aware that everything is going to be so much more fun and much easier if you have a support team, or at least one enthusiastic friend or family member, to help on the day. Even if this person is an expert in their field, you've still got to be sure that he or she will be a help, not a hindrance. It doesn't matter how good a competitor your friend is herself; if she is spending her time winding up you and your horse and distracting you, she won't help you to be successful or make it an enjoyable experience.

Each of us have different requirements when preparing for a show; when you're feeling nervous you might need a little bit of understanding from those around you. Someone might be hilarious at a party with their jokes and impressions, but they probably won't be the ideal helper now. Personally, I go pretty quiet when I'm concentrating, so I wouldn't want someone with me who wanted to chat just as I'm going into the ring (although this might be relaxing for someone else—we're all individuals, after all).

You also need someone who won't get offended when you ask them to do things. If it's muddy, you're going to need your boots wiped before going into a showing class (it's a good idea to do the bottom of your boots anyway to make sure you're feet don't slip), and you can't do this yourself. Sometimes it's easier to ask family to do this, rather than paid help. If you do go for paid help, make sure they totally understand what they're expected to do and that they do get some time off, too. If all else fails, and you've no one to come with you, you could always advertise for help at your local tack shop. I've heard of something similar working: "Show groom required. Very high status position (no pay), beverages and sandwiches supplied. Get fit and breathe in lovely fresh air supporting my horse and I as we attempt some shows this summer. Please call…"

Something came up with my 24-year-old daughter the other day while she was talking about some of her classmates. She made the comment, "You know, they have NO IDEA how to deal with a stressful situation…" And I sat back and mulled it over—and she's right, you know; one of the most important things that competing teaches you in the long term is how to cope with stress. If you've learnt to swallow your nerves and keep calm while waiting for that crucial jumping round (or flat class), then you can apply the same techniques to the exam room, and that job interview, and the important phone calls. She has a catchphrase from a book, "Feel the fear and do it anyway."

SADIE

Get ready, set, go…

Full preparations might start the day or the month before, but certainly all the preparations for the next day should have been made by 6pm the evening before. Please don't leave anything until the last minute! You ought to know exactly how you're getting to the show the next day and have all your horse's clothing, feed, water and equipment clean and ready to go. Always contact your farrier in good time to make sure that your horse's shoes (if he wears them) are in good order, and find out whether your horse needs special studs in his shoes for the going. If so, check that you know how to change them. Have your riding clothes ready the night before: everything you wear should be as comfortable and safe as possible. It doesn't matter that your jodhpurs cost a fortune or are the latest color; if they're not comfortable, they have to go!

It might sound odd to you, but as you choose your clothes for the competition, you should think about which ones will best help you to stay at the right temperature while you are riding. Shaking with cold is not conducive to confident riding, and neither is sweating from too many clothes. Being clean and well dressed will help you feel better about yourself and shows a respect for the competition organizers. Don't wear anything you haven't ridden in before; riding in the wrong underwear is enough to put anyone off riding for life! Some people get clammy hands when competing, so get comfortable with wearing lightweight gloves when riding, and always have a spare pair available in case you lose one or both. (By wearing gloves you can avoid the symptoms reminding you that you're nervous.)

It's much harder to feel confident when you're in any way physically below par. Many people feel their stomachs churning when they're apprehensive. Find out what are the most suitable foods for you to eat before competing, then stick to those. When going away to a horse show, take your own food with you, upset stomachs are common amongst those who have only eaten a burger all day. Have some Pepto Bismol, or a similar stomach-calming remedy, on hand should you need it.

If your digestion seems generally bad and you find yourself craving foods that make it worse, see a good nutritionist. There are many ways to improve this (just as with horses): chromium can help to stabilize blood sugar levels and reduce sugar cravings, magnesium can ease chocolate

▽ *"Once men are caught up in an event they cease to be afraid." Antoine de Saint-Exupéry*

Competition can make the world a better place for animals and people

The Brooke is the world's leading equine welfare charity, which aims to improve the lives of horses, donkeys and mules working in the poorest parts of the world. These animals are the backbone of the economy in many developing countries; supporting countless poor communities where many people earn less than a dollar a day.

Millions of loyal working animals endure untold suffering (much of which is entirely preventable) and when an animal becomes ill or even dies, its owner and their family are left vulnerable and destitute.

However, there can be a happier and healthier future for these animals and the millions of poor families that rely on them. The Brooke's mobile veterinary teams and animal health workers, together with its partner organizations worldwide, help by providing free veterinary treatment and training to owners across 9 countries in Asia, Africa, Central America and the Middle East.

"Happy Donkey" competition

At this event in India, more than 30 children between the ages of 8 to 14 brought their donkeys to be assessed by the Brooke team. All the children were eager to demonstrate how well they look after their donkeys.

Salman, aged 8, won the first prize and told Brooke India staff: "My donkey won the first prize! I keep my donkey clean and healthy. My donkey makes sure we have money always, and I am very happy with Brooke doctors—they come to my home and check on my donkey and show my family how to keep him happy. That's why I won this competition."

Abbas, a Brooke Community Animal Health Worker, explains that, "When we started our animal welfare project in Gadaipuri we found the donkeys were weak, injured and suffering from diseases—mainly caused by malnutrition, and being overloaded and overworked. So the idea for the competition evolved from a group meeting with the children and it seemed an effective way of encouraging them to be sensitive towards their animals. As a result, the children have become more aware of the importance of welfare."

A Brooke Hospital for Animals poll showed that when most of us think of equine animals we think they are "beautiful" (45 percent), "powerful" (35 percent), "fast" (35 percent) and "strong" (34 percent). But these are attributes we would find hard to apply to the 90 million working animals that struggle day in, day out, in some of the harshest environments in the world. For the millions of people who depend on them—these are the world's real equine heroes.

cravings, Evening Primrose or Borage Oil (high GLA) are good for hormonal changes—so get to know your remedies!

Even if nerves mean you're not hungry, eat at least one hour before your class. If you are competing in several classes, make sure you eat and drink at appropriate times so you don't suddenly feel weak.

Aim to arrive at the showground at least 2 hours before your class so you have time to relax and prepare both yourself and your horse. There is nothing worse than a last-minute rush.

If you are competing in a jumping competition, it is good advice to walk the course very carefully (I'd even suggest this if you're riding in a race). Always walk the line you intend to ride and never cut corners when you are walking. This is not the time for socializing and chatting to your friends and fellow competitors, apart from seeing that the ground is good on the track you intend to ride, this is your chance to get a proper view of the fences you are going to be approaching—in this situation, no surprise is a good thing!

Be considerate of your horse's needs at shows: he should be driven there carefully and needs ventilation and light when in the horse trailer; he should also be offered water regularly and it doesn't harm him to nibble some forage on the way either. We always transport our horses with haylage or well-soaked hay, as it is healthier for the horse if you reduce the inevitable dust as much as possible when traveling. Think carefully about where you are going to park when you arrive at the show—will your horse be best off if you park somewhere away from the others, should you find him a shady spot? Or do you want to arrive early to get the best view of the ring so you can watch from the trailer? (Tip: Always be *especially* charming to the parking attendants so they'll be more prepared to help you out!) Don't have your horse clipped out fully before the show then leave him standing outside the trailer without a blanket and freezing (I've seen this at shows), and don't leave him in a baking-hot trailer, or tied up in full sunlight on a hot day, either.

Don't measure your success purely in terms of ribbons won. A long-term plan is the best way to go, so instead see how much you and your horse are improving at each show.

Always thank the stewards, judges and show secretary at the end of the day—even if you didn't win! They have a very long day; it's hard work and being thanked is often their only reward for giving up their time.

THE OLDER RIDER

I rode a bit as a child and although I adored horses I was always nervous. I stopped riding at 14 then started again at 18, when I ended up with a horse going down on his knees with me on a tarmac road (he'd done this before, I later learned). I awoke to find myself surrounded by motorists and an ambulance and lost my nerve. I tried to ride on family holidays but my fear was completely unmanageable, so I didn't ride again for over 30 years.

Then one day a friend persuaded me to accompany her. I got the bug again and went again and again. My husband then surprised me by buying a horse I had been riding at the riding center. I told him he was crazy and that I could not do this, but it was too late as the deal had already been done!

One day I heard that Kelly Marks was doing a demonstration in Rambouillet, France, not far from where I lived. I went along and made the decision to go on a weekend course by Kelly and Nicole Golding. The first time I went I just watched and then the next time, aged 57, I actually took part with the horses.

After that I saw Monty at Solihull and joined the Intelligent Horsemanship Association. After watching Kelly and Monty work I decided to take up riding as seriously as I had taken work as a clinical psychologist before my retirement. This was an important decision and I gave it my all.

This has been a major life change for me. As I learned to "read" my horse and think about my own responses, I found a way of managing my fear. From a psychologists standpoint, I think the key here is observation, observation, observation. Child psychotherapists and psychoanalysts spend hours observing newborns and young children in their "natural habitats" before they start their clinical work, then they write up the interactions, observe in detail and discuss them in seminars over years.

In the weekends that I spent with Kelly and Nicole I learned to observe the "signs" and the placement of the body and to read the horse's own language. It gave me confidence and kept me calm; I was able to manage a situation and to stay still or move appropriately and then I was able to work with my own mare. I had a great fear, but nowadays I know I can handle it.

Some five years later I have learned to jump, won in the over 25s at 3' in the Dordogne, jumped at the French National Championships and bred two foals.

The two crucial things were the courses and demonstrations followed by slogging day in, day out to gain the knowledge—including doing my French riding exams so I was eligible to compete. I'm never going to be a great rider, I may have left it just a little too late (I'm 63 now), but I never dreamed I could get this far, nor that my life could change so much.

MARILYN PIETRONI

Prayer power!

So now we're completely versed in visualization/affirmations/positive thinking and then one day we're in a situation and we think, "It's no good; this time I'm definitely and without doubt going to die." What then?

Believe me, I've been there—and at totally curious times. For instance, before I went on the French trip where I eventually met Monty, I had a deep foreboding, a feeling of dread; I didn't know what was going to happen, but I knew it was going to be something awful! Things were also so bad the night before my second Ladies' European Championship that I actually wrote goodbye letters to people: "If anything should happen to me on this trip I want you to know how much I've loved you and what a bonus you have been in my life…" So how positive was *that*?!

If you can dream and not make dreams your Master
If you can think and not make thoughts your aim
If you can meet with Triumph and Disaster
And treat those two imposters just the same.

RUDYARD KIPLING

I do know for certain that in both those situations there was a point when I actually prayed. By praying I mean that I asked "someone" for help. You don't have to be in any special place for this (although if you do have a special quiet place, then that's ideal), but the important thing is to find the quiet, still place in your head, take a moment to ask for the help you need and then just leave it up to whichever higher power you've asked.

Now this is a big subject, and probably way beyond the scope of this book, but let me just say how it works for me. From my formal religious education I learnt that the most important part of this is "let *thy* will be done." This means that God/the universe/whoever isn't *obliged* to do as you ask, but only to consider it within the scope of their other plans. When I've prayed I tend to feel a terrific sense of relief—it makes me feel that I can continue doing the best that I can, but I don't have to worry about trying to control things or "make" something happen because basically it's in someone else's hands now. In more New Age terms this act would be called "releasing" or "letting go," and there are many testimonials to the fact that it can make an enormous difference in people's lives. If nothing else, you're now no longer trying so hard that you're actually blocking things from happening.

I think many of us are very frugal with our prayers because, well, I guess we "don't want to impose," but maybe it's something we should practice more?

Prayer or faith?

When I was 18, one of the top dealers in my area asked me if I'd ride for him in competition. I really needed something good to turn up in my life at that time and this was a dream opportunity.

The first two classes I rode in were a real disaster, though. I was eliminated in one class and had 20 faults in the next. I felt terrible. As ever, there was a fair bit of jealousy along the lines of, "Who is she to get this top job?" And there were a few people around who delighted in telling the dealer what a bad choice he'd made. I knew this, and I felt so guilty for letting him down that I said, "Look, I really understand if you don't want me to ride for you any more…" But he wouldn't hear of it. "You're going to be all right," he said. He had more faith in me than I did!

Every morning until the following weekend I'd wake up far too early feeling sick and I would lie awake repeating positive affirmations as best I could (but I still felt sick). I didn't get another opportunity to ride for the dealer until I was due to compete again on the Saturday, and as I rode Summerfield James into the first class at Windsor Great Park a little group gathered to watch, and I knew it wasn't because they were wishing me well. There was a big part of me that felt sure James was going to stop at the first, but I remember saying a prayer to some "higher power" asking, "Just let me do the best I'm capable of." I was determined to give it my best effort.

I remember saying, "Come on, James!" as we went into the first. He not only cleared that fence beautifully but the rest of the course, too, and he was the fastest clear in the jump off. In an amazing turnaround we won

Endurance pays off

Gazing out at the early morning landscape of the Cevennes mountains in Southern France I thought, "What more could a girl want?" As I sunk in among the saddle and the dogs in the back of a two-seater, four-wheel drive, I felt relaxed. I was meditating on the moment: the company and warmth of two friends and teammates, and the anticipation of a long-held dream that was about to be fulfilled. In a few hours I would be riding a 12 ½ mile endurance race on a beautiful Arabian horse.

But the night before I hadn't been at all relaxed and dinner felt like the last supper. I was nervous and tense thinking of all that could go wrong. I had only sat on the Arab stallion I was about to ride, Papyrus du Desert (Papinou or Pappy for short), for the first time just days before. We hadn't even ridden out together, and although he was lovely, he also had a reputation for being a bit hot and headstrong—particularly around other horses. I prayed we would make it around the course safely, and if we actually qualified, that would be more than amazing.

Thankfully I woke up relaxed and focused on the day of the race. One of my best memories of that morning was setting off, just Pappy and me. We had to keep a pace of 7 ½ an hour which meant getting round in 1 hour 45 minutes (I used my cell phone as a timer). The results of the race would be calculated on the basis of the

contender's riding speed, divided by the average speed of the course (as ridden by all competitors), multiplied by the eventual heart rate of the horse. Pacing the race and keeping the horse as calm as possible would be key.

Papinou had run and qualified before so he was diligent and responsive on the trail, but he also possessed an intense blend of bravado and anxiety, and he feared horses approaching him from behind. I tried to keep him away from other riders, and we ran most of the race at a trot and canter. He was beautifully balanced and the trail was exquisite; shady soft tracks through leafy woods and the occasional road crossing.

I met up with my teammates, Alain and Corrine, at these crossings. They'd pass up water (some of which I'd use to soak Pappy's neck) and give advice such as: "Look where you're going; follow the red arrows!" (I had taken a momentary wrong turn earlier.) I smiled at their advice, happy that *I* was the rider this time—not the wistful assistant I had been in the past.

Towards the end of the course we had a team chat about my time and I checked my mobile: 2 minutes 45 seconds to go. I held a steady pace until sighting the finish line and then we glided into a canter and past the officials.

Pappy passed the vet test, his heart rate was good and he was sound and well hydrated. When I told the vet it had been my first race she was pleased for me because, subject to our timing being correct, we had probably qualified.

As I walked back to the trailer with Alain and Pappy, I felt a surge of emotion—and tears followed. It was relief mixed in with a deep respect and gratitude for the horse and my team.

At the prize-giving ceremony 5 hours later they announced the 8 qualifiers in reverse order. I was worried when they got to third place and my name still hadn't been called. I thought that maybe we hadn't qualified after all.

But we had won! We went home with a ridiculously big trophy and a host of goodies for the horse, beaming like Cheshire Cats. Our happiness really felt complete when we finally watched Papinou rolling in his paddock, back from a good day's work safe and sound.

Endurance racing is popular in the US as well as France, so here are some tips I've put together if you want to give it a try:

- Know your horse's character—his strengths and weaknesses—and develop a good partnership by keeping him safe and reassured.
- Be relaxed, but keep your rhythm and focus.
- Gradually increase your riding pace, leaving enough time to slow down towards the end. This helps the heart rate.
- Dress sensibly and comfortably.
- Don't ride to win; it could serve as a distraction.
- Always do the best thing for yourself and your horse; don't feel obliged to be sociable, and ask people to pass you when required.
- Don't mistake endurance racing for trail riding—it's a lot more demanding and an organized, capable team is essential.
- Train yourself so you can stay upright and balanced for the duration of the race.
- Enjoy it. It's a fantastic way to spend time with horses and people.

MICHELE DANAN, MONTY ROBERTS
PRELIMINARY CERTIFICATE HOLDER

ASSIGNMENT
Don't let fear hold you back

Give yourself an hour before you go to sleep tonight to write down all the experiences you had when you were the person you are most proud of being. Yes, you may have felt fear at the time, but you didn't let it hold you back: you went in with heart beating and you did it. (Admit it, you're a hero!)

Consult not your fears but your hopes and your dreams.

POPE JOHN XXIII

both the classes we were entered in that day. (If ever life seems too good to be true, don't worry about it—treasure it!) I stayed with that owner for a wonderful 2 seasons before I left showjumping to go into racing.

I'm not sure what made the difference that day—was it the prayer? Was it knowing that the owner had faith that I could do it? Looking back I realize he knew far more about what I was capable of than I did. It was a wonderful gift he gave me; there are plenty of people out there who need convincing that they're not "broken" and they need to be put back together in this way in order to become something decent. All they need is for someone like him to reveal the wonderfulness that's already there.

Although we're discouraged (quite rightly) from just sitting around and waiting for our knight in shining armor, it's amazing how it sometimes just takes one person to believe you are something special to completely turn your life around. I have to admit to being "rescued" like that once or twice, and I remember my eyes welling up with tears when someone remarked about Pie, "He knows he's special, doesn't he?" I hope that all those important people in my life "know they're special."

That event at Windsor helped me to realize that miracles do happen, and if ever I'm in a situation where I'm terrified (nervousness is for wimps! *I* get "terrified"!). I think back to that sunny day in June and I can feel the exact same emotions. Coming up to that first fence, I remember the thought, "This can't be done'" and then, "Yes, it can!"

Have you ever had an experience like that? Was there a time when you really didn't think you could achieve something, but you did? It doesn't have to be in the context of horses or a competition; it could have been when confronting a bully, or helping someone who had hurt himself when you always thought you were squeamish. Go right back to that feeling now. Become completely immersed in this. Some people call this "accessing a state"—remember it, you may need to call on this state again if you find you particularly need courage and calmness for something in the future.

Ignorance is bliss?

Although I don't always agree with the above statement, I do remember a time when I was race riding in Belgium when my trainer appeared in an agitated state as I walked into the parade ring.

He was chain-smoking even faster than normal and his eyes seemed to be bulging out of his head; he gripped my arm and said, "Now, Kelly, just because this is the biggest Tierce of the year, you mustn't let it worry you. This mare could win but if you get panicking because it's a Tierce it'll ruin all her chances." And I was thinking, "What's a Tierce?" He said, "Just because this race is worth 400,000 francs—don't even think about that! It would be crazy to have that on your mind. Listen, Kelly," then he went on slowly, "just ride this race like it's a perfectly normal race and don't even think about it being worth 400,000 francs." And I was thinking, "I wonder how much 400,000 francs is in real money?" I was starting to believe this race might be really quite important but my grey cells (we were in Belgium, home of Poirot, after all) were trying to work out—so if it's 11 francs to the pound, does that make it…? Luckily, that must have kept me occupied during the race because I managed not to interfere with the mare enough to let her win by a head. The trainer was beside himself with joy when I came in and praised me for being so cool on this, the biggest race of his career!

European Ladies' Championship in Vienna

I had always wanted to win a championship. In the years that I had been a contender in the British Ladies' races I would generally finish fifth on points every year. When I considered that I was working from a stable that generally had a choice of 8 horses for me to ride, whereas some of the other riders were competing from stables with over 150 horses, I was really very lucky to be in contention at all, and actually winning a championship looked like an impossibility.

There was a Ladies European Championship every year when each European country would send one of their top lady riders out to compete, and so I was delighted in 1994 when I was chosen to represent Britain. I don't mind telling you that I really, really, really wanted to win—it would have been a dream come true for me (particularly as I was near retirement time as a jockey, because there comes a time in your life when you know it's time to "move on").

The last word on competition

Having a competition to enter could be the ideal concrete goal if you would like to measure the progress of yourself and your horse. Choose the right competition and make sure you work on the right attitude and all this will ensure that the pair of you really benefit from the day and enjoy yourselves.

I don't find it comfortable to want something so much, especially when I know that it's in the lap of the gods anyway. The horses we were going to ride were to be drawn for us in a ballot, so we would only get to see them as we went out to the paddock to get on them for the race. The champion would be the rider who gained the most points over four races.

Things went really well and I won one race and was third and fourth in another. The points were counted up at the end and I finished second overall. So close! Although I had really, really wanted to win, it was OK: I felt good to have been part of it all and I knew I'd given it my best effort. Of course it was disappointing, but you learn (or you need to) that in life some disappointment is part of the package. Deal with it!

So that was that. I still continued to ride in the odd few races, but I was getting more involved with Monty Roberts and his work and at this stage. I was mainly working with racehorses with fears of going in the starting stalls, and I knew that my ambitions didn't lie in training

When it's best to keep quiet!

Some race trainers are very aware of how important the "last words" the jockey hears are as he goes onto the racecourse. These careful trainers will often therefore lead their horse out of the parade paddock themselves, rather than let the jockey do it and face being "sabotaged" by some thoughtless person who comes out to the racecourse with them and gives them different instructions or a last-minute warning that really isn't going to help.

▷ *My brother Geoffrey leading me up in the parade ring.*

racehorses. My father was not going to continue training much longer, but in August the following year I was asked to ride a horse at Newmarket for another trainer. If you know a little about racing you'll know that in a handicap race each horse is allotted a weight based on his past performance. In other words, the more a horse wins the more weight he has to carry until he loses a few races and then they take a few pounds off his back (weights in the saddle) each time. This horse I was going to ride was a little filly, she couldn't have been any more than 15hh, and because she had run well in two of her last three races she was having to carry over 150 pounds in this race—an enormous weight for her.

I keep a diary and that night I wrote in it the trainer's instructions to me. As I listened to them I started to feel that I was involved in something distasteful. As I rode the horse down to the start I could feel her mouth was really sore, and I felt so sorry for her. I'm pleased to say that I didn't follow the trainer's instructions and we finished down the field. The trainer was furious when I came in from the race and, as I wrote up my diary, he said, "I told you to hit her HARD 5 times, what the **** did you think you were doing?"

I felt incredibly depressed after that experience and I'm not sure I did know what I thought I was doing. I noted in my diary, too, "I went and visited Max and Sam Maxwell that evening. Most of all I needed to be around some horses. Sam and Max were very understanding. They made me a drink as I sat, rather shell–shocked, trying to make sense of how some people treat horses,"

I knew it was the end of the line as far as my racing was concerned, but it was a pretty sad note to end on. Later that evening I'd agreed to go out to dinner with some of our British team riders and some of the foreign girls who were over, and Joanna Winter asked if she could have a word with me. Jo had been chosen to ride in the European Ladies' Championship that year (1995) and was due to go the next week. I don't know what was happening in her life at that time, but for some reason she had doubts about going. She's always been a good friend to me and she said, "I'll decline and ask that you go in my place." Because I wanted to do the "right" thing I was saying, "Jo, you've got to go, it's such a terrific opportunity. I loved it last time, honestly, you've got to go," but when she finally convinced me it was not what she wanted to do, I felt, "YES"

It was a bit like déjà vu. I so, so wanted to win—although this time I knew that if I lost, as I'd already proved, I could live with it. In the first race I had to carry a very low weight (this horse hadn't won for a *very* long time!)

▽ A positive attitude may not solve all your problems, but it will annoy enough people to make it worth the effort.

which meant a tiny saddle. I finished third, which wasn't bad considering the saddle was slipping during most of the race. Then the next race I won.

We had dinner that night (which I couldn't eat because I had to keep very light) and traveled to another racecourse for the 2 races the next day. In my diary it says, "I was trying to find a phone to call someone at home. I'm actually in the lead and I want to savor this moment to the maximum!" I wasn't expecting to stay in the lead, though. It's hard to describe my feelings the next day when I saw the horse I was due to ride in the first race. If I said to you "Imagine you're going on a blind date and you're a bit apprehensive about what he's going to be like. And then they bring through George Clooney…" this might give you some idea! I looked at this simply *gorgeous* horse they brought into the paddock and I thought, "How can a girl get this lucky?"

We won by 3 lengths. That win put me so far ahead on points that in the last race I only had to keep breathing to win the Championship. I stood on the winner's rostrum and they played "God Save the Queen." What a moment! Strangely, I felt an overwhelming relief that I would never have to ride in a race again. I had a strong feeling that a whole new life lay ahead of me…

△ *Was this the end for me? Or was it, in fact, just a new beginning?*

Index

Acknowledgements

I've certainly had some wonderful 'success buddies' working with me on this book, Nicole Golding of www.whisperingback.co.uk was my consultant editor. Nicole is an author in her own right, and due to her own self-development journey she was not only about to contribute a host of positive things to this book but to my life in general – for which I'm extremely grateful. Then there's my psychologist friend Wendy Kendall (of www.allowchange.com). It's rather handy when you're writing a book like this to have a friend with a First in Behavioural Sciences (Anthropology, Sociology and Psychology – with her major being Psychology), and a Masters degree in Applied Psychology! Wendy contributed as well as critique and helped to ensure the suggestions within the book are all responsible and workable. Also, I couldn't have had better help from Ebury with design by Isobel Gillan, editing from Helena Caldon and with, as always, support from Carey Smith and Sarah Lavelle.

I'd like to thank those fantastic charities www.veteran-horse-society.co.uk and www.thebrooke.org for their photographs and for the wonderful work they do – please visit their websites to learn more.

I'd like to thank all the Intelligent Horsemanship Recommended Associates who, through the wonderful reports I have about them virtually every day, give me heaps of confidence that we're going in the right direction to help horses and their owners too. My office support team, Brenda Whelehan, Gitte Monahan, Linda Dibbens, Shaun Whelehan and Bridget Taylor are wonderful as always. I'm very grateful to all those who have contributed stories and for the work of the enormously talented photographers throughout this book. As ever, I wish to thank Monty Roberts who has been the best mentor anyone could wish for and also those who I have mentored who give me the thrill of knowing this work can go on and we really can make a difference. I'd like to thank Kate Fox (author of the wonderful *Watching the English*) for her encouraging words and Phillip Cross for reading the manuscript and saying 'he walked away a more confident person' afterwards – and also for sending me photos (not just of horses) to keep me cheerful when I was getting a bit bogged down. I am grateful to my life-enhancing friend Angela Vince who has managed to keep me in touch with the real world, and my lovely non-horsey mother who was the one who said to my father all those years ago, 'It's time Kelly had her own pony'.

And, finally, I mustn't forget someone enormously important in my life: that's 'my boy' Pie – he's all the fun I imagined having a horse could be.

Useful Addresses

For information on Intelligent Horsemanship courses, demonstrations, shopping, personal help with your horse or your own confidence issues and our recommended reading list please see our website:
www.intelligenthorsemanship.co.uk

or write to:
Kelly Marks
Intelligent Horsemanship
Lethornes
Lambourn
Berkshire
RG17 8QS
(United Kingdom)

Telephone (+44) 01488 71300
or fax (+44) 01488 73783

Picture Credits

The Random House Group would like to thank the following for providing photographs and permission to reproduce copyright material. While every effort has been made to trace and acknowledge all copyright holders, we would like to apologize should there have been any errors or omissions.

All images by Matthew Webb apart from the following:
Mark J Barrett 19, 20, 69, 79, 85, 91, 130–1, 145, 154, 175; Roberto Battistini 116;
Corbis 12, 30, 32, 54, 59, 99, 113, 184, 185, 200, 205, 214; Cotswold Photography 191;
Cristy Cumberworth 196; Eventer Photography 159; Ian Gorton 167; Kit Houghton 36, 108;
Bob Langrish 47; Matthew Morgan 156, 193; Simon Palmer 191, 194; Amit Pasricha/ Brooke 207;
Max Pickering/Maximagery.com 39, 50, 53, 78, 118, 121, 142, 146, 150, 181;
Real Time Imaging Picture 89, 148; Monty and Pat Roberts Inc. Archives 25;
Skyla Consultants 23; Sabine Stuewer 8, 66, 172; Juliet van Otteren 224;
Veteran Horse Site/Daily Mail 178; Jess Wallace 35